Wittgenstein on Rules
and Private Language

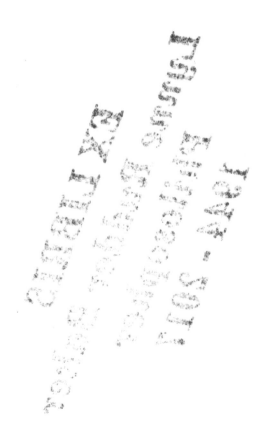

SAUL A. KRIPKE

Wittgenstein on Rules and Private Language

An Elementary Exposition

Harvard University Press
Cambridge, Massachusetts

Copyright © 1982 by Saul A. Kripke

All rights reserved

SEVENTH PRINTING, 1994

Printed in the United States of America

Library of Congress Cataloging in Publication Data

Kripke, Saul A., 1940–

Wittgenstein on rules and private language.

Includes bibliographical references and index.
Wittgenstein, Ludwig, 1889–1951.   I. Title
B3376.W564K74   192   81-20070
                                                  AACR2

ISBN 0-674-95401-7 (paper)

Contents

(

To my parents

Preface

The main part of this work has been delivered at various places as lectures, series of lectures, or seminars. It constitutes, as I say, 'an elementary exposition' of what I take to be the central thread of Wittgenstein's later work on the philosophy of language and the philosophy of mathematics, including my interpretation of the 'private language argument', which on my view is principally to be explicated in terms of the problem of 'following a rule'. A postscript presents another problem Wittgenstein saw in the conception of private language, which leads to a discussion of some aspects of his views on the problem of other minds. Since I stress the strong connection in Wittgenstein's later philosophy between the philosophy of psychology and the philosophy of mathematics, I had hoped to add a second postscript on the philosophy of mathematics. Time has not permitted this, so for the moment the basic remarks on philosophy of mathematics in the main text must suffice.

The present work is hardly a commentary on Wittgenstein's later philosophy, nor even on *Philosophical Investigations*. Many well known and significant topics – for example, the idea of 'family resemblances', the concept of 'certainty' – are hardly mentioned. More important, in the philosophy of mind itself, a wealth of material, such as Wittgenstein's views on intention, memory, dreaming, and the like, are barely glanced at. It is my hope that much of this material becomes fairly clear from an understanding of Wittgenstein's view of the central topic.

Many of Wittgenstein's views on the nature of sensations and sensation language are either only glanced at or are omitted altogether; and, as is stressed in the text, I adopted the deliberate policy of avoiding discussion of those sections following §243 of the *Investigations* that are ordinarily called the 'private language argument'. I think that many of these sections – for example, §§258ff. – become much clearer when they are read in the light of the main argument of the present work; but probably some of the exegetical puzzles in some of these sections (e.g. §265) are not devoid of residue. The interest of these sections is real, but in my view their importance should not be overstressed, since they represent special cases of a more general argument. Usually I presented this work to sophisticated philosophers, but it is my hope that introductory classes in Wittgenstein could use it in conjunction with other material. In classes it would be helpful especially for the instructor to try out the Wittgensteinian paradox on the group, and to see what solutions are proposed. Here primarily I mean responses to the paradox that we follow the rule as we do without reason or justification, rather than the philosophical theories (dispositions, qualitative states, etc.), discussed later in the same chapter. It is important for the student to feel the problem intuitively. I recommend the same initial emphasis to readers who propose to study the present work on their own. I also recommend that the student (re)read the *Investigations* in the light of the structuring of the argument proposed in this work. Such a procedure is of special importance here, since largely my method is to present the argument as it struck me, as it presented a problem for me, rather than to concentrate on the exegesis of specific passages.

Since I first encountered the 'private language argument' and the later Wittgenstein generally, and since I came to think about it in the way expounded here (1962–3), his work on rules has occupied a more central position in discussions of

Wittgenstein's later work. (It had been discussed to some extent all along.) Some of this discussion, especially that appearing after I gave my London, Ontario lecture, can be presumed to have been influenced by the present exposition, but some of it, in and out of print, can be presumed to be independent. I have not tried to cite similar material in the literature, partly because if I made the attempt, I would be certain to slight some published work and even more, some unpublished work. I have become satisfied, for reasons mentioned below in the text and footnotes, that publication still is not superfluous.

It deserves emphasis that I do not in this piece of writing attempt to speak for myself, or, except in occasional and minor asides, to say anything about my own views on the substantive issues. The primary purpose of this work is the presentation of a problem and an argument, not its critical evaluation. Primarily I can be read, except in a few obvious asides, as almost like an attorney presenting a major philosophical argument as it struck me. If the work has a main thesis of its own, it is that Wittgenstein's sceptical problem and argument are important, deserving of serious consideration.

Various people, including at least Rogers Albritton, G. E. M. Anscombe, Irving Block, Michael Dummett, Margaret Gilbert, Barbara Humphries, Thomas Nagel, Robert Nozick, Michael Slote, and Barry Stroud, influenced this essay. In addition to the Wittgenstein Conference in London, Ontario, 1976, I gave various versions of this material as Howison Lectures, the University of California, Berkeley, 1977; as a series of lectures in a special colloquium held in Banff, Alberta, 1977; and at a Wittgenstein Conference held at Trinity College, Cambridge, England, 1978. Versions were also given in seminars at Princeton University, the first being in the Spring Term of 1964–5. Only in these Princeton seminars did I have time to include the material in the postscript, so that it has had less benefit of discussion and reaction from others than the rest. No doubt I was influenced by the discussion of my argument at these conferences and seminars. I should especially like to thank Steven Patten and Ron Yoshida for their beautifully prepared transcripts of the Banff version, and Irving Block both for his help as editor of the volume in which an earlier version of this work appeared, and for inviting me to make this exposition more public at the London Conference. *Samizdat* transcripts of the version given at the London Conference have been circulated widely in Oxford and elsewhere.

An earlier version of the work appeared in I. Block (ed.), *Perspectives on the Philosophy of Wittgenstein* (Basil Blackwell, Oxford, 1981, xii + 322 pp.). Work on that version was partially supported by a Guggenheim Fellowship, by a Visiting Fellowship at All Souls College, Oxford, by a sabbatical from Princeton University, and by the National Science Foundation (USA). Work on the present expanded version was partially supported by a grant from the American Council of Learned Societies, by a sabbatical from Princeton University, and by an Oscar Ewing Research Grant at Indiana University.

I

Introductory

Wittgenstein's celebrated argument against 'private language' has been discussed so often that the utility of yet another exposition is certainly open to question. Most of the exposition which follows occurred to the present writer some time ago, in the academic year 1962–3. At that time this approach to Wittgenstein's views struck the present writer with the force of a revelation: what had previously seemed to me to be a somewhat loose argument for a fundamentally implausible conclusion based on dubious and controversial premises now appeared to me to be a powerful argument, even if the conclusions seemed even more radical and, in a sense, more implausible, than before. I thought at that time that I had seen Wittgenstein's argument from an angle and emphasis very different from the approach which dominated standard expositions. Over the years I came to have doubts. First of all, at times I became unsure that I could formulate Wittgenstein's elusive position as a clear argument. Second, the elusive nature of the subject made it possible to interpret some of the standard literature as perhaps seeing the argument in the same way after all. More important, conversations over the years showed that, increasingly, others were seeing the argument with the emphases I preferred. Nevertheless, recent expositions by very able interpreters differ enough from the following to make me think that a new exposition may still be of use.[1]

A common view of the 'private language argument' in *Philosophical Investigations* assumes that it begins with section 243, and that it continues in the sections immediately following.[2] This view takes the argument to deal primarily with a problem about 'sensation language'. Further discussion of the argument in this tradition, both in support and in criticism, emphasizes such questions as whether the argument invokes a form of the verification principle, whether the form in question is justified, whether it is applied correctly to sensation language, whether the argument rests on an exaggerated scepticism about memory, and so on. Some

[1] Looking through some of the most distinguished commentaries on Wittgenstein of the last ten or fifteen years, I find some that still treat the discussion of rules cursorily, virtually not at all, as if it were a minor topic. Others, who discuss both Wittgenstein's views on the philosophy of mathematics and his views on sensations in detail, treat the discussion of rules as if it were important for Wittgenstein's views on mathematics and logical necessity but separate it from 'the private language argument'. Since Wittgenstein has more than *one* way of arguing for a given conclusion, and even of presenting a single argument, to defend the present exegesis I need not necessarily argue that these other commentaries are in error. Indeed, they may give important and illuminating expositions of facets of the *Investigations* and its argument deemphasized or omitted in this essay. Nevertheless, in emphasis they certainly differ considerably from the present exposition.

[2] Unless otherwise specified (explicitly or contextually), references are to *Philosophical Investigations*. The small numbered units of the *Investigations* are termed 'sections' (or 'paragraphs'). Page references are used only if a section reference is not possible, as in the second part of the *Investigations*. Throughout I quote the standard printed English translation (by G. E. M. Anscombe) and make no attempt to question it except in a very few instances. *Philosophical Investigations* (x+232 pp., parallel German and English text) has undergone several editions since its first publication in 1953 but the paragraphing and pagination remain the same. The publishers are Basil Blackwell, Oxford and Macmillan, New York.

This essay does not proceed by giving detailed exegesis of Wittgenstein's text but rather develops the arguments in its own way. I recommend that the reader reread the *Investigations* in the light of the present exegesis and see whether it illuminates the text.

crucial passages in the discussion following §243 – for example, such celebrated sections as §258 and §265 – have been notoriously obscure to commentators, and it has been thought that their proper interpretation would provide the key to the 'private language argument'.

In my view, the real 'private language argument' is to be found in the sections *preceding* §243. Indeed, in §202 *the conclusion is already stated explicitly*: "Hence it is not possible to obey a rule 'privately': otherwise thinking one was obeying a rule would be the same thing as obeying it." I do not think that Wittgenstein here thought of himself as *anticipating* an argument he was to give in greater detail later. On the contrary, the crucial considerations are all contained in the discussion leading up to the conclusion stated in §202. The sections following §243 are meant to be read in the light of the preceding discussion; difficult as they are in any case, they are much less likely to be understood if they are read in isolation. The 'private language argument' as applied to *sensations* is only a special case of much more general considerations about language previously argued; sensations have a crucial role as an (apparently) convincing *counterexample* to the general considerations previously stated. Wittgenstein therefore goes over the ground again in this special case, marshalling new specific considerations appropriate to it. It should be borne in mind that *Philosophical Investigations* is not a systematic philosophical work where conclusions, once definitely established, need not be reargued. Rather the *Investigations* is written as a perpetual dialectic, where persisting worries, expressed by the voice of the imaginary interlocutor, are never definitively silenced. Since the work is not presented in the form of a deductive argument with definitive theses as conclusions, the same ground is covered repeatedly, from the point of view of various special cases and from different angles, with the hope that the entire process will help the reader see the problems rightly.

The basic structure of Wittgenstein's approach can be presented briefly as follows: A certain problem, or in Humean terminology, a 'sceptical paradox', is presented concerning the notion of a rule. Following this, what Hume would have called a 'sceptical solution' to the problem is presented. There are two areas in which the force, both of the paradox and of its solution, are most likely to be ignored, and with respect to which Wittgenstein's basic approach is most likely to seem incredible. One such area is the notion of a mathematical rule, such as the rule for addition. The other is our talk of our own inner experience, of sensations and other inner states. In treating both these cases, we should bear in mind the basic considerations about rules and language. Although Wittgenstein has already discussed these basic considerations in considerable generality, the structure of Wittgenstein's work is such that the special cases of mathematics and psychology are not simply discussed by citing a general 'result' already established, but by going over these special cases in detail, in the light of the previous treatment of the general case. By such a discussion, it is hoped that both mathematics and the mind can be seen rightly: since the temptations to see them wrongly arise from the neglect of the same basic considerations about rules and language, the problems which arise can be expected to be analogous in the two cases. In my opinion, Wittgenstein did not view his dual interests in the philosophy of mind and the philosophy of mathematics as interests in two separate, at best loosely related, subjects, as someone might be interested both in music and in economics. Wittgenstein thinks of the two subjects as involving the same basic considerations. For this reason, he calls his investigation of the foundations of mathematics "analogous to our investigation of psychology" (p. 232). It is no accident that essentially the same basic material on rules is included in both *Philosophical Investigations* and in *Remarks on the Foundations of Mathematics*,[3] both times as

---

[3] Basil Blackwell, Oxford, 1956, xix+204 pp. In the first edition of *Remarks on the Foundations of Mathematics* the editors assert (p. vi) that Wittgenstein appears originally to have intended to include some of the material on mathematics in *Philosophical Investigations*.

The third edition (1978) includes more material than earlier editions

the basis of the discussions of the philosophies of mind and of mathematics, respectively, which follow.

In the following, I am largely trying to present Wittgenstein's argument, or, more accurately, that set of problems and arguments which I personally have gotten out of reading Wittgenstein. With few exceptions, I am *not* trying to present views of my own; neither am I trying to endorse or to criticize Wittgenstein's approach. In some cases, I have found a precise statement of the problems and conclusions to be elusive. Although one has a strong sense that there is a problem, a rigorous statement of it is difficult. I am inclined to think that Wittgenstein's later philosophical style, and the difficulty he found (see his Preface) in welding his thought into a conventional work presented with organized arguments and conclusions, is not simply a stylistic and literary preference, coupled with a *penchant* for a certain degree of obscurity,[4] but stems in part from the nature of his subject.[5]

I suspect – for reasons that will become clearer later – that to attempt to present Wittgenstein's argument precisely is to some extent to falsify it. Probably many of my formulations and recastings of the argument are done in a way Wittgenstein would not himself approve.[6] So the present paper should be thought of as expounding neither 'Wittgenstein's' argument nor 'Kripke's': rather Wittgenstein's argument as it struck Kripke, as it presented a problem for him.

As I have said, I think the basic 'private language argument' *precedes* section 243, though the sections following 243 are no

---

and rearranges some of the sections and divisions of earlier editions. When I wrote the present work, I used the first edition. Where the references differ, the equivalent third edition reference is given in square brackets.

[4] Personally I feel, however, that the role of stylistic considerations here cannot be denied. It is clear that purely stylistic and literary considerations meant a great deal to Wittgenstein. His own stylistic preference obviously contributes to the difficulty of his work as well as to its beauty.

[5] See the discussion of this point in pages 69–70 below.

[6] See again the same discussion in pages 69–70.

doubt of fundamental importance as well. I propose to discuss the problem of 'private language' initially without mentioning these latter sections *at all*. Since these sections are often thought to *be* the 'private language argument', to some such a procedure may seem to be a presentation of Hamlet without the prince. Even if this is so, there are many other interesting characters in the play.[7]

[7] Looking over what I have written below, I find myself worried that the reader may lose the main thread of Wittgenstein's argument in the extensive treatment of finer points. In particular, the treatment of the dispositional theory below became so extensive because I heard it urged more than once as an answer to the sceptical paradox. That discussion may contain somewhat more of Kripke's argumentation in support of Wittgenstein rather than exposition of Wittgenstein's own argument than does most of the rest of this essay. (See notes 19 and 24 for *some* of the connections. The argument is, however, inspired by Wittgenstein's original text. Probably the part with the least direct inspiration from Wittgenstein's text is the argument that our dispositions, like our actual performance, are not potentially infinite. Even this, however, obviously has its origin in Wittgenstein's parallel emphasis on the fact that we explicitly think of only finitely many cases of any rule.) The treatment below (pp. 38–39) of simplicity is an example of an objection that, as far as I know, Wittgenstein never considers himself. I think that my reply is clearly appropriate, assuming that I have understood the rest of Wittgenstein's position appropriately. I urge the reader to concentrate, on a first reading, on understanding the intuitive force of Wittgenstein's sceptical problem and to regard byways such as these as secondary.

2

The Wittgensteinian Paradox

In §201 Wittgenstein says, "this was our paradox: no course of action could be determined by a rule, because every course of action can be made out to accord with the rule." In this section of the present essay, in my own way I will attempt to develop the 'paradox' in question. The 'paradox' is perhaps the central problem of *Philosophical Investigations*. Even someone who disputes the conclusions regarding 'private language', and the philosophies of mind, mathematics, and logic, that Wittgenstein draws from his problem, might well regard the problem itself as an important contribution to philosophy. It may be regarded as a new form of philosophical scepticism.

Following Wittgenstein, I will develop the problem initially with respect to a mathematical example, though the relevant sceptical problem applies to all meaningful uses of language. I, like almost all English speakers, use the word 'plus' and the symbol '+' to denote a well-known mathematical function, addition. The function is defined for all pairs of positive integers. By means of my external symbolic representation and my internal mental representation, I 'grasp' the rule for addition. One point is crucial to my 'grasp' of this rule. Although I myself have computed only finitely many sums in the past, the rule determines my answer for indefinitely many new sums that I have never previously considered. This is the whole point of the notion that in learning to add I grasp a rule: my past intentions regarding addition determine a unique answer for indefinitely many new cases in the future.

Let me suppose, for example, that '68 + 57' is a computation that I have never performed before. Since I have performed – even silently to myself, let alone in my publicly observable behavior – only finitely many computations in the past, such an example surely exists. In fact, the same finitude guarantees that there is an example exceeding, in both its arguments, all previous computations. I shall assume in what follows that '68 + 57' serves for this purpose as well.

I perform the computation, obtaining, of course, the answer '125'. I am confident, perhaps after checking my work, that '125' is the correct answer. It is correct both in the arithmetical sense that 125 is the sum of 68 and 57, and in the metalinguistic sense that 'plus', as I intended to use that word in the past, denoted a function which, when applied to the numbers I called '68' and '57', yields the value 125.

Now suppose I encounter a bizarre sceptic. This sceptic questions my certainty about my answer, in what I just called the 'metalinguistic' sense. Perhaps, he suggests, as I used the term 'plus' in the past, the answer I intended for '68+57' should have been '5'! Of course the sceptic's suggestion is obviously insane. My initial response to such a suggestion might be that the challenger should go back to school and learn to add. Let the challenger, however, continue. After all, he says, if I am now so confident that, as I used the symbol '+', my intention was that '68+57' should turn out to denote 125, this cannot be because I explicitly gave myself instructions that 125 is the result of performing the addition in this particular instance. By hypothesis, I did no such thing. But of course the idea is that, in this new instance, I should apply the very same function or rule that I applied so many times in the past. But who is to say what function this was? In the past I gave myself only a finite number of examples instantiating this function. All, we have supposed, involved numbers smaller than 57. So perhaps in the past I used 'plus' and '+' to denote a function which I will call 'quus' and symbolize by '⊕'. It is defined by:

$$x \oplus y = x+y, \text{ if } x, y < 57$$
$$= 5 \quad \text{otherwise.}$$

Who is to say that this is not the function I previously meant by '+'?

The sceptic claims (or feigns to claim) that I am now misinterpreting my own previous usage. By 'plus', he says, I *always meant* quus;[8] now, under the influence of some insane frenzy, or a bout of LSD, I have come to misinterpret my own previous usage.

Ridiculous and fantastic though it is, the sceptic's hypothesis is not logically impossible. To see this, assume the common sense hypothesis that by '+' I *did* mean addition. Then it would be *possible*, though surprising, that under the influence of a momentary 'high', I should misinterpret all my past uses of the plus sign as symbolizing the quus function, and proceed, in conflict with my previous linguistic intentions, to compute 68 plus 57 as 5. (I would have made a mistake, not in mathematics, but in the supposition that I had accorded with my previous linguistic intentions.) The sceptic is proposing that I have made a mistake precisely of this kind, but with a plus and quus reversed.

Now if the sceptic proposes his hypothesis sincerely, he is crazy; such a bizarre hypothesis as the proposal that I always meant quus is absolutely wild. Wild it indubitably is, no doubt it is false; but if it is false, there must be some fact about my past usage that can be cited to refute it. For although the hypothesis is wild, it does not seem to be *a priori* impossible.

8 Perhaps I should make a remark about such expressions as "By 'plus' I meant quus (or plus)," "By 'green' I meant green," etc. I am not familiar with an accepted felicitous convention to indicate the object of the verb 'to mean'. There are two problems. First, if one says, "By 'the woman who discovered radium' I meant the woman who discovered radium," the object can be interpreted in two ways. It may stand for a woman (Marie Curie), in which case the assertion is true only if 'meant' is used to mean referred to (as it can be used); or it may be used to denote the *meaning* of the quoted expression, not a woman, in which case the assertion is true

Of course this bizarre hypothesis, and the references to LSD, or to an insane frenzy, are in a sense merely a dramatic ⌐device. The basic point is this. Ordinarily, I suppose that, in computing '68+57' as I do, I do not simply make an unjustified leap in the dark. I follow directions I previously gave myself that uniquely determine that in this new instance I should say '125'. What are these directions? By hypothesis, I never explicitly told myself that I should say '125' in this very instance. Nor can I say that I should simply 'do the same thing

––––––––––

with 'meant' used in the ordinary sense. Second, as is illustrated by 'referred to', 'green', 'quus', etc. above, as objects of 'meant', one must use various expressions as objects in an awkward manner contrary to normal grammar. (Frege's difficulties concerning unsaturatedness are related.) Both problems tempt one to put the object in quotation marks, like the subject; but such a usage conflicts with the convention of philosophical logic that a quotation denotes the expression quoted. Some special 'meaning marks', as proposed for example by David Kaplan, could be useful here. If one is content to ignore the first difficulty and always use 'mean' to mean denote (for most purposes of the present paper, such a reading would suit at least as well as an intensional one; often I speak as if it is a *numerical function* that is meant by plus), the second problem might lead one to nominalize the objects – 'plus' denotes the plus function, 'green' denotes greenness, etc. I contemplated using italics ("'plus' means *plus*"; "'mean' may mean *denote*"), but I decided that normally (except when italics are otherwise appropriate, especially when a neologism like 'quus' is introduced for the first time), I will write the object of 'to mean' as an ordinary roman object. The convention I have adopted reads awkwardly in the written language but sounds rather reasonable in the spoken language.

Since use–mention distinctions are significant for the argument as I give it, I try to remember to use quotation marks when an expression is mentioned. However, quotation marks are also used for other purposes where they might be invoked in normal non-philosophical English writing (for example, in the case of " 'meaning marks' " in the previous paragraph, or " 'quasi-quotation' " in the next sentence). Readers familiar with Quine's 'quasi-quotation' will be aware that in some cases I use ordinary quotation where logical purity would require that I use quasi-quotation or some similar device. I have not tried to be careful about this matter, since I am confident that in practice readers will not be confused.

I always did,' if this means 'compute according to the rule exhibited by my previous examples.' That rule could just as well have been the rule for quaddition (the quus function) as for addition. The idea that in fact quaddition *is* what I meant, that in a sudden frenzy I have changed my previous usage, dramatizes the problem.

In the discussion below the challenge posed by the sceptic takes two forms. First, he questions whether there is any *fact* that I meant plus, not quus, that will answer his sceptical challenge. Second, he questions whether I have any reason to be so confident that now I should answer '125' rather than '5'. The two forms of the challenge are related. I am confident that I should answer '125' because I am confident that this answer also accords with what I *meant*. Neither the accuracy of my computation nor of my memory is under dispute. So it ought to be agreed that *if* I meant plus, then unless I wish to change my usage, I am justified in answering (indeed compelled to answer) '125', not '5'. An answer to the sceptic must satisfy two conditions. First, it must give an account of what fact it is (about my mental state) that constitutes my meaning plus, not quus. But further, there is a condition that any putative candidate for such a fact must satisfy. It must, in some sense, show how I am justified in giving the answer '125' to '68 + 57'. The 'directions' mentioned in the previous paragraph, that determine what I should do in each instance, must somehow be 'contained' in any candidate for the fact as to what I meant. Otherwise, the sceptic has not been answered when he holds that my present response is arbitrary. Exactly how this condition operates will become much clearer below, after we discuss Wittgenstein's paradox on an intuitive level, when we consider various philosophical theories as to what the fact that I meant plus might consist in. There will be many specific objections to these theories. But all fail to give a candidate for a fact as to what I meant that would show that only '125', not '5', is the answer I 'ought' to give.

The ground rules of our formulation of the problem should be made clear. For the sceptic to converse with me at all, we must have a common language. So I am supposing that the sceptic, provisionally, is not questioning my *present* use of the word 'plus'; he agrees that, according to my *present* usage, '68 plus 57' denotes 125. Not only does he agree with me on this, he conducts the entire debate with me in my language as I *presently* use it. He merely questions whether my present usage agrees with my past usage, whether I am *presently* conforming to my *previous* linguistic intentions. The problem is not "How do I know that 68 plus 57 is 125?", which should be answered by giving an arithmetical computation, but rather "How do I know that '68 plus 57', as I *meant* 'plus' in the *past*, should denote 125?" If the word 'plus' as I used it in the past, denoted the quus function, not the plus function ('quaddition' rather than addition), then my *past* intention was such that, asked for the value of '68 plus 57', I should have replied '5'.

I put the problem in this way so as to avoid confusing questions about whether the discussion is taking place 'both inside and outside language' in some illegitimate sense.[9] If we are querying the meaning of the word 'plus', how can we use it (and variants, like 'quus') at the same time? So I suppose that the sceptic assumes that he and I agree in our *present* uses of the word 'plus': we both use it to denote addition. He does *not* – at least initially – deny or doubt that addition is a genuine function, defined on all pairs of integers, nor does he deny that we can speak of it. Rather he asks why I now believe that by 'plus' in the *past*, I meant addition rather than quaddition. If I meant the former, then to accord with my previous usage I should say '125' when asked to give the result of calculating '68 plus 57'. If I meant the latter, I should say '5'.

The present exposition tends to differ from Wittgenstein's original formulations in taking somewhat greater care to make explicit a distinction between use and mention, and between questions about present and past usage. About the present example Wittgenstein might simply ask, "How do I know that I should respond '125' to the query '68+57'?" or "How do

---

[9] I believe I got the phrase "both inside and outside language" from a conversation with Rogers Albritton.

I know that '68 + 57' comes out 125?" I have found that when the problem is formulated this way, some listeners hear it as a sceptical problem about *arithmetic*: "How do I know that 68 + 57 is 125?" (Why not answer this question with a mathematical proof?) At least at this stage, scepticism about arithmetic should not be taken to be in question: we may assume, if we wish, that 68 + 57 *is* 125. Even if the question is reformulated 'metalinguistically' as "How do I know that 'plus', as I use it, denotes a function that, when applied to 68 and 57, yields 125?", one may answer, "Surely I know that 'plus' denotes the plus function and accordingly that '68 plus 57' denotes 68 plus 57. But if I know arithmetic, I know that 68 plus 57 is 125. So I know that '68 plus 57' denotes 125!" And surely, if I use language at all, I cannot doubt coherently that 'plus', as I now use it, denotes plus! Perhaps I cannot (at least at this stage) doubt this about my *present* usage. But I can doubt that my *past* usage of 'plus' denoted plus. The previous remarks – about a frenzy and LSD – should make this quite clear.

Let me repeat the problem. The sceptic doubts whether any instructions I gave myself in the past compel (or justify) the answer '125' rather than '5'. He puts the challenge in terms of a sceptical hypothesis about a change in my usage. Perhaps when I used the term 'plus' in the *past*, I always meant quus: by hypothesis I never gave myself any explicit directions that were incompatible with such a supposition.

Of course, ultimately, if the sceptic is right, the concepts of meaning and of intending one function rather than another will make no sense. For the sceptic holds that no fact about my past history – nothing that was ever in my mind, or in my external behavior – establishes that I meant plus rather than quus. (Nor, of course, does any fact establish that I meant quus!) But if this is correct, there can of course be no fact about which function I meant, and if there can be no fact about which particular function I meant in the *past*, there can be none in the *present* either. But before we pull the rug out from under our own feet, we begin by speaking as if the notion that at present we mean a certain function by 'plus' is unquestioned and unquestionable. Only past usages are to be questioned. Otherwise, we will be unable to *formulate* our problem.

Another important rule of the game is that there are no limitations, in particular, no *behaviorist* limitations, on the facts that may be cited to answer the sceptic. The evidence is not to be confined to that available to an external observer, who can observe my overt behavior but not my internal mental state. It would be interesting if nothing in my external behavior could show whether I meant plus or quus, but something about my inner state could. But the problem here is more radical. Wittgenstein's philosophy of mind has often been viewed as behavioristic, but to the extent that Wittgenstein may (or may not) be hostile to the 'inner', no such hostility is to be assumed as a premise; it is to be argued as a conclusion. So whatever 'looking into my mind' may be, the sceptic asserts that even if God were to do it, he still could not determine that I meant addition by 'plus'.

This feature of Wittgenstein contrasts, for example, with Quine's discussion of the 'indeterminacy of translation'.[10] There are many points of contact between Quine's discussion and Wittgenstein's. Quine, however, is more than content to assume that only behavioral evidence is to be admitted into his discussion. Wittgenstein, by contrast, undertakes an extensive introspective[11] investigation, and the results of the investiga-

---

[10] See W. V. Quine, *Word and Object* (MIT, The Technology Press, Cambridge, Massachusetts, 1960, xi + 294 pp.), especially chapter 2, 'Translation and Meaning' (pp. 26–79). See also *Ontological Relativity and Other Essays* (Columbia University Press, New York and London, 1969, viii + 165 pp.), especially the first three chapters (pp. 1–90); and see also "On the Reasons for the Indeterminacy of Translation," *The Journal of Philosophy*, vol. 67 (1970), pp. 178–83.
     Quine's views are discussed further below, see pp. 55–7.
[11] I do not mean the term 'introspective' to be laden with philosophical doctrine. Of course much of the baggage that has accompanied this term would be objectionable to Wittgenstein in particular. I simply mean that he makes use, in his discussion, of our own memories and knowledge of our 'inner' experiences.

tion, as we shall see, form a key feature of his argument. Further, the way the sceptical doubt is presented is not behavioristic. It is presented from the 'inside'. Whereas Quine presents the problem about meaning in terms of a linguist, trying to guess what someone *else* means by his words on the basis of his behavior, Wittgenstein's challenge can be presented to me as a question about *myself*: was there some past fact about me – what I 'meant' by plus – that mandates what I should do now?

To return to the sceptic. The sceptic argues that when I answered '125' to the problem '68 + 57', my answer was an unjustified leap in the dark; my past mental history is equally compatible with the hypothesis that I meant quus, and therefore should have said '5'. We can put the problem this way: When asked for the answer to '68 + 57', I unhesitatingly and automatically produced '125', but it would seem that if previously I never performed this computation explicitly I might just as well have answered '5'. Nothing justifies a brute inclination to answer one way rather than another.

Many readers, I should suppose, have long been impatient to protest that our problem arises only because of a ridiculous model of the instruction I gave myself regarding 'addition'. Surely I did not merely give myself some finite number of examples, from which I am supposed to extrapolate the whole table ("Let '+' be the function instantiated by the following examples: . . ."). No doubt infinitely many functions are compatible with *that*. Rather I learned – and internalized instructions for – a *rule* which determines how addition is to be continued. What was the rule? Well, say, to take it in its most primitive form: suppose we wish to add *x* and *y*. Take a huge bunch of marbles. First count out *x* marbles in one heap. Then count out *y* marbles in another. Put the two heaps together and count out the number of marbles in the union thus formed. The result is *x* + *y*. This set of directions, I may suppose, I explicitly gave myself at some earlier time. It is engraved on my mind as on a slate. It is incompatible with the hypothesis that I meant quus. It is this set of directions, not the finite list of particular additions I performed in the past, that justifies and determines my present response. This consideration is, after all, reinforced when we think what I really *do* when I add 68 and 57. I do not reply automatically with the answer '125' nor do I consult some non-existent past instructions that I should answer '125' in this case. Rather I proceed according to an *algorithm* for addition that I previously learned. The algorithm is more sophisticated and practically applicable than the primitive one just described, but there is no difference in principle.

Despite the initial plausibility of this objection, the sceptic's response is all too obvious. True, if 'count', as I used the word in the past, referred to the act of counting (and my other past words are correctly interpreted in the standard way), then 'plus' must have stood for addition. But I applied 'count', like 'plus', to only finitely many past cases. Thus the sceptic can question my present interpretation of my past usage of 'count' as he did with 'plus'. In particular, he can claim that by 'count' I formerly meant *quount*, where to 'quount' a heap is to count it in the ordinary sense, unless the heap was formed as the union of two heaps, one of which has 57 or more items, in which case one must automatically give the answer '5'. It is clear that if in the past 'counting' meant quounting, and if I follow the rule for 'plus' that was quoted so triumphantly to the sceptic, I must admit that '68+57' must yield the answer '5'. Here I have supposed that previously 'count' was never applied to heaps formed as the union of sub-heaps either of which has 57 or more elements, but if this particular upper bound does not work, another will do. For the point is perfectly general: if 'plus' is explained in terms of 'counting', a non-standard interpretation of the latter will yield a non-standard interpretation of the former.[12]

---

[12] The same objection scotches a related suggestion. It might be urged that the quus function is ruled out as an interpretation of '+' because it fails to satisfy some of the laws I accept for '+' (for example, it is not associative; we could have defined it so as not even to be commutative). One might even observe that, on the natural numbers, addition is the only function that satisfies certain laws that I accept – the 'recursion equations' for +: $(x$

It is pointless of course to protest that I intended the result of counting a heap to be *independent* of its composition in terms of sub-heaps. Let me have said this to myself as explicitly as possible: the sceptic will smilingly reply that once again I am misinterpreting my past usage, that actually 'independent' formerly meant *quindependent*, where 'quindependent' means . . .

Here of course I am expounding Wittgenstein's well-known remarks about "a rule for interpreting a rule". It is tempting to answer the sceptic by appealing from one rule to another more 'basic' rule. But the sceptical move can be repeated at the more 'basic' level also. Eventually the process must stop – "justifications come to an end somewhere" – and I am left with a rule which is completely unreduced to any other. How can I justify my present application of such a rule, when a sceptic could easily interpret it so as to yield any of an indefinite number of other results? It seems that my application of it is an unjustified stab in the dark. I apply the rule *blindly*.

Normally, when we consider a mathematical rule such as addition, we think of ourselves as *guided* in our application of it to each new instance. Just this is the difference between someone who computes new values of a function and someone who calls out numbers at random. Given my past intentions regarding the symbol '+', one and only one answer

---

$(x+\mathrm{o}=x)$ and (x) (y) $(x+y'=(x+y)')$ where the stroke or dash indicates successor; these equations are sometimes called a 'definition' of addition. The problem is that the other signs used in these laws (the universal quantifiers, the equality sign) have been applied in only a finite number of instances, and they can be given non-standard interpretations that will fit non-standard interpretations of '+'. Thus for example '(x)' might mean for every $x < h$, where h is some upper bound to the instances where universal instantiation has hitherto been applied, and similarly for equality.

In any event the objection is somewhat overly sophisticated. Many of us who are not mathematicians use the '+' sign perfectly well in ignorance of any explicitly formulated laws of the type cited. Yet surely we use '+' with the usual determinate meaning nonetheless. What justifies us applying the function as we do?

is dictated as the one appropriate to '68+57'. On the other hand, although an intelligence tester may suppose that there is only one possible continuation to the sequence 2, 4, 6, 8, . . ., mathematical and philosophical sophisticates know that an indefinite number of rules (even rules stated in terms of mathematical functions as conventional as ordinary polynomials) are compatible with any such finite initial segment. So if the tester urges me to respond, after 2, 4, 6, 8, . . ., with *the* unique appropriate next number, the proper response is that no such unique number exists, nor is there any unique (rule determined) infinite sequence that continues the given one. The problem can then be put this way: Did I myself, in the directions for the future that I gave myself regarding '+', really differ from the intelligence tester? True, I may not merely stipulate that '+' is to be a function instantiated by a finite number of computations. In addition, I may give myself directions for the further computation of '+', stated in terms of other functions and rules. In turn, I may give myself directions for the further computation of these functions and rules, and so on. Eventually, however, the process must stop, with 'ultimate' functions and rules that I have stipulated for myself only by a *finite* number of examples, just as in the intelligence test. If so, is not my procedure as arbitrary as that of the man who guesses the continuation of the intelligence test? In what sense is my actual computation procedure, following an algorithm that yields '125', more justified by my past instructions than an alternative procedure that would have resulted in '5'? Am I not simply following an unjustifiable impulse?[13]

13 Few readers, I suppose, will by this time be tempted to appeal a determination to "go on the same way" as before. Indeed, I mention it at this point primarily to remove a possible misunderstanding of the sceptical argument, not to counter a possible reply to it. Some followers of Wittgenstein – perhaps occasionally Wittgenstein himself – have thought that his point involves a rejection of 'absolute identity' (as opposed to some kind of 'relative' identity). I do not see that this is so, whether or not doctrines of 'relative' identity are correct on other grounds. Let identity be as 'absolute' as one pleases: it holds only between

Of course, these problems apply throughout language and are not confined to mathematical examples, though it is with mathematical examples that they can be most smoothly brought out. I think that I have learned the term 'table' in such a way that it will apply to indefinitely many future items. So I can apply the term to a new situation, say when I enter the Eiffel Tower for the first time and see a table at the base. Can I answer a sceptic who supposes that by 'table' in the past I meant *tabair*, where a 'tabair' is anything that is a table not found at the base of the Eiffel Tower, or a chair found there? Did I think explicitly of the Eiffel Tower when I first 'grasped the concept of' a table, gave myself directions for what I meant by 'table'? And even if I did think of the Tower, cannot any directions I gave myself mentioning it be reinterpreted compatibly with the sceptic's hypothesis? Most important

---

each thing and itself. Then the plus function is identical with itself, and the quus function is identical with itself. None of this will tell me whether I referred to the plus function or to the quus function in the past, nor therefore will it tell me which to use in order to apply the same function now.

Wittgenstein does insist (§§215–16) that the law of identity ('everything is identical with itself') gives no way out of this problem. It should be clear enough that this is so (whether or not the maxim should be rejected as 'useless'). Wittgenstein sometimes writes (§§225–27) as if the way we give a response in a new case determines what we call the 'same', as if the meaning of 'same' varies from case to case. Whatever impression this gives, it need not relate to doctrines of relative and absolute identity. The point (which can be fully understood only after the third section of the present work) can be put this way: If someone who computed '+' as we do for small arguments gave bizarre responses, in the style of 'quus', for larger arguments, and insisted that he was 'going on the same way as before', we would not acknowledge his claim that he was 'going on in the same way' as for the small arguments. What we call the 'right' response determines what we call 'going on in the same way'. None of this in itself implies that identity is 'relative' in senses that 'relative identity' has been used elsewhere in the literature.

In fairness to Peter Geach, the leading advocate of the 'relativity' of identity, I should mention (lest the reader assume I had him in mind) that he is *not* one of those I have heard expound Wittgenstein's doctrine as dependent on a denial of 'absolute' identity.

for the 'private language' argument, the point of course
applies to predicates of sensations, visual impressions, and the
like, as well: "*How do I know* that in working out the series + 2
I must write "20,004, 20,006" and not "20,004, 20,008"? – (The
question: "How do I know that this color is 'red'?" is
similar.)" (*Remarks on the Foundations of Mathematics*, I, §3.) The
passage strikingly illustrates a central thesis of this essay: that
Wittgenstein regards the fundamental problems of the philosophy of mathematics and of the 'private language argument'
– the problem of sensation language – as at root identical,
stemming from his paradox. The whole of §3 is a succinct and
beautiful statement of the Wittgensteinian paradox; indeed the
whole initial section of part I of *Remarks on the Foundations
of Mathematics* is a development of the problem with special
reference to mathematics and logical inference. It has been
supposed that all I need to do to determine my use of the word
'green' is to have an image, a sample, of green that I bring to
mind whenever I apply the word in the future. When I use this
to justify my application of 'green' to a new object, should not
the sceptical problem be obvious to any reader of Goodman?[14]
Perhaps by 'green', in the past I meant *grue*,[15] and the color
image, which indeed was grue, was meant to direct me to
apply the word 'green' to *grue* objects always. If the *blue* object
before me now is grue, then it falls in the extension of 'green',
as I meant it in the past. It is no help to suppose that in the past I
stipulated that 'green' was to apply to all and only those things
'of the same color as' the sample. The sceptic can reinterpret
'same color' as same *schmolor*,[16] where things have the same
schmolor if . . .

---

[14] See Nelson Goodman, *Fact, Fiction, and Forecast* (3rd ed., Bobbs-Merrill,
Indianapolis, 1973, xiv + 131 pp.), especially ch. III, §4, pp. 72–81.

[15] The exact definition of 'grue' is unimportant. It is best to suppose that
past objects were grue if and only if they were (then) green while present
objects are grue if and only if they are (now) blue. Strictly speaking, this is
not Goodman's original idea, but it is probably most convenient for
present purposes. Sometimes Goodman writes this way as well.

[16] 'Schmolor', with a slightly different spelling, appears in Joseph Ullian,
"More on 'Grue' and Grue," *The Philosophical Review*, vol. 70 (1961),
pp. 386–9.

Let us return to the example of 'plus' and 'quus'. We have just summarized the problem in terms of the basis of my present particular response: what tells me that I should say '125' and not '5'? Of course the problem can be put equivalently in terms of the sceptical query regarding my present intent: nothing in my mental history establishes whether I meant plus or quus. So formulated, the problem may appear to be epistemological – how can anyone know which of these I meant? Given, however, that everything in my mental history is compatible both with the conclusion that I meant plus and with the conclusion that I meant quus, it is clear that the sceptical challenge is not really an epistemological one. It purports to show that nothing in my mental history of past behavior – not even what an omniscient God would know – could establish whether I meant plus or quus. But then it appears to follow that there was no *fact* about me that constituted my having meant plus rather than quus. How could there be, if nothing in my internal mental history or external behavior will answer the sceptic who supposes that in fact I meant quus? If there was no such thing as my meaning plus rather than quus in the past, neither can there be any such thing in the present. When we initially presented the paradox, we perforce used language, taking present meanings for granted. Now we see, as we expected, that this provisional concession was indeed fictive. There can be no fact as to what I mean by 'plus', or any other word at any time. The ladder must finally be kicked away.

This, then, is the sceptical paradox. When I respond in one way rather than another to such a problem as '68 + 57', I can have no justification for one response rather than another. Since the sceptic who supposes that I meant quus cannot be answered, there is no fact about me that distinguishes between my meaning plus and my meaning quus. Indeed, there is no fact about me that distinguishes between my meaning a definite function by 'plus' (which determines my responses in new cases) and my meaning nothing at all.

Sometimes when I have contemplated the situation, I have had something of an eerie feeling. Even now as I write, I feel

confident that there is something in my mind – the meaning I
attach to the 'plus' sign – that *instructs* me what I ought to do in
all future cases. I do not *predict* what I *will* do – see the
discussion immediately below – but instruct myself what I
ought to do to conform to the meaning. (Were I now to make a
prediction of my future behavior, it would have substantive
content only because it already makes sense, in terms of the
instructions I give myself, to ask whether my intentions will
be conformed to or not.) But when I concentrate on what is
now in my mind, what instructions can be found there? How
can I be said to be acting on the basis of these instructions when
I act in the future? The infinitely many cases of the table are not
in my mind for my future self to consult. To say that there is a
general rule in my mind that tells me how to add in the future
is only to throw the problem back on to other rules that also
seem to be given only in terms of finitely many cases. What
can there be in my mind that I make use of when I act in the
future? It seems that the entire idea of meaning vanishes into
thin air.

Can we escape these incredible conclusions? Let me first
discuss a response that I have heard more than once in
conversation on this topic. According to this response, the
fallacy in the argument that no fact about me constitutes my
meaning plus lies in the assumption that such a fact must
consist in an *occurrent* mental state. Indeed the sceptical
argument shows that my entire occurrent past mental history
might have been the same whether I meant plus or quus, but
all this shows is that the fact that I meant plus (rather than
quus) is to be analyzed *dispositionally*, rather than in terms of
occurrent mental states. Since Ryle's *The Concept of Mind*,
dispositional analyses have been influential; Wittgenstein's
own later work is of course one of the inspirations for such
analyses, and some may think that he himself wishes to
suggest a dispositional solution to his paradox.

The dispositional analysis I have heard proposed is simple.
To mean addition by '+' is to be disposed, when asked for any
sum '$x+y$' to give the sum of x and y as the answer (in

particular, to say '125' when queried about '68+57'); to mean quus is to be disposed when queried about any arguments, to respond with their *quum* (in particular to answer '5' when queried about '68+57'). True, my actual thoughts and responses in the past do not differentiate between the plus and the quus hypotheses; but, even in the past, there were dispositional facts about me that did make such a differentiation. To say that in fact I meant plus in the past is to say – as surely was the case! – that had I been queried about '68 + 57', I *would* have answered '125'. By hypothesis I was not in fact asked, but the disposition was present none the less.

To a good extent this reply immediately ought to appear to be misdirected, off target. For the sceptic created an air of puzzlement as to my *justification* for responding '125' rather than '5' to the addition problem as queried. He thinks my response is no better than a stab in the dark. Does the suggested reply advance matters? How does it *justify* my choice of '125'? What it says is: " '125' is the response you are disposed to give, and (perhaps the reply adds) it would also have been your response in the past." Well and good, I know that '125' is the response I am disposed to give (I am actually giving it!), and maybe it is helpful to be told – as a matter of brute fact – that I would have given the same response in the past. How does any of this indicate that – now *or* in the past – '125' was an answer *justified* in terms of instructions I gave myself, rather than a mere jack-in-the-box unjustified and arbitrary response? Am I supposed to justify my present belief that I meant addition, not quaddition, and hence should answer '125', in terms of a *hypothesis* about my *past* dispositions? (Do I record and investigate the past physiology of my brain?) Why am I so sure that one particular hypothesis of this kind is correct, when all my past thoughts can be construed either so that I meant plus or so that I meant quus? Alternatively, is the hypothesis to refer to my *present* dispositions alone, which would hence give the right answer by definition?

Nothing is more contrary to our ordinary view – or

Wittgenstein's – than is the supposition that "whatever is going to seem right to me is right." (§258). On the contrary, "that only means that here we can't talk about right" (*ibid.*). A candidate for what constitutes the state of my meaning one function, rather than another, by a given function sign, ought to be such that, whatever in fact I (am disposed to) do, there is a unique thing that I *should* do. Is not the dispositional view simply an equation of performance and correctness? Assuming determinism, even if I mean to denote *no* number theoretic function in particular by the sign '$\star$', then to the same extent as it is true for '$+$', it is true here that for any two arguments m and n, there is a uniquely determined answer p that I would give.[17] (I choose one at random, as we would normally say, but causally the answer is determined.) The difference between this case and the case of the '$+$' function is that in the former case, but not in the latter, my uniquely determined answer can properly be called 'right' or 'wrong'.[18]

So it does seem that a dispositional account misconceives the sceptic's problem – to find a past fact that *justifies* my present response. As a candidate for a 'fact' that determines what I mean, it fails to satisfy the basic condition on such a candidate, stressed above on p. 11, that it should *tell* me what I ought to do in each new instance. Ultimately, almost all objections to the dispositional account boil down to this one. However, since the dispositionalist does offer a popular

[17] We will see immediately below that for arbitrarily large m and n, this assertion is not really true even for '$+$'. That is why I say that the assertion is true for '$+$' and the meaningless '$\star$' 'to the same extent'.

[18] I might have introduced '$\star$' to mean nothing in particular even though the answer I arbitrarily choose for '$m \star n$' is, through some quirk in my brain structure, uniquely determined independently of the time and other circumstances when I am asked the question. It might, in addition, even be the case that I consciously resolve, once I have chosen a particular answer to '$m \star n$', to stick to it if the query is repeated for any particular case, yet nevertheless I think of '$\star$' as meaning no function in particular. What I will not say is that my particular answer is 'right' or 'wrong' in terms of the *meaning* I assigned to '$\star$', as I will for '$+$', since there is no such meaning.

candidate for what the fact as to what I mean might be, it is worth examining some problems with the view in more detail.

As I said, probably some have read Wittgenstein himself as favoring a dispositional analysis. I think that on the contrary, although Wittgenstein's views have dispositional elements, any such analysis is inconsistent with Wittgenstein's view.[19]

[19] Russell's *The Analysis of Mind* (George Allen and Unwin, London, in the Muirhead Library of Philosophy, 310 pp.) already gives dispositional analyses of certain mental concepts: see especially, Lecture III, "Desire and Feeling," pp. 58–76. (The object of a desire, for example, is roughly defined as that thing which, when obtained, will cause the activity of the subject due to the desire to cease.) The book is explicitly influenced by Watsonian behaviorism; see the preface and the first chapter. I am inclined to conjecture that Wittgenstein's philosophical development was influenced considerably by this work, both in the respects in which he sympathizes with behavioristic and dispositional views, and to the extent that he opposes them. I take *Philosophical Remarks* (Basil Blackwell, Oxford, 1975, 357 pp., translated by R. Hargreaves and R. White), §§21ff., to express a rejection of Russell's theory of desire, as stated in Lecture III of *The Analysis of Mind*. The discussion of Russell's theory played, I think, an important role in Wittgenstein's development: the problem of the relation of a desire, expectation, etc., to its object ('intentionality') is one of the important forms Wittgenstein's problem about meaning and rules takes in the *Investigations*. Clearly the sceptic, by proposing his bizarre interpretations of what I previously meant, can get bizarre results as to what (in the present) does, or does not, satisfy my past desires or expectations, or what constitutes obedience to an order I gave. Russell's theory parallels the dispositional theory of meaning in the text by giving a causal dispositional account of desire. Just as the dispositional theory holds that the value I meant '+' to have for two particular arguments *m* and *n* is, by definition, the answer I would give if queried about '*m+n*', so Russell characterizes the thing I desired as the thing which, were I to get it, would quiet my 'searching' activity. I think that even in the *Investigations*, as in *Philosophical Remarks* (which stems from an earlier period), Wittgenstein still rejects Russell's dispositional theory because it makes the relation between a desire and its object an 'external' relation (*PR*, §21), although in the *Investigations*, unlike *Philosophical Remarks*, he no longer bases this view on the 'picture theory' of the *Tractatus*. Wittgenstein's view that the relation between the desire (expectation, etc.) and its object must be 'internal', not 'external',

First, we must state the simple dispositional analysis. It gives a criterion that will tell me what number theoretic function φ I mean by a binary function symbol 'f', namely: The referent φ of 'f' is that unique binary function φ such that I am disposed, if queried about '$f(m, n)$', where 'm' and 'n' are numerals denoting particular numbers m and n, to reply 'p', where 'p' is a numeral denoting $\varphi(m, n)$. The criterion is meant to enable us to 'read off' which function I mean by a given function symbol from my disposition. The cases of addition and quaddition above would simply be special cases of such a scheme of definition.[20]

The dispositional theory attempts to avoid the problem of the finiteness of my actual past performance by appealing to a disposition. But in doing so, it ignores an obvious fact: not only my actual performance, but also the totality of my dispositions, is finite. It is not true, for example, that if queried about the sum of any two numbers, no matter how large, I will reply with their actual sum, for some pairs of numbers are

parallels corresponding morals drawn about meaning in my text below (the relation of meaning and intention to future action is 'normative, not descriptive', p. 37 below). Sections 429–65 discuss the fundamental problem of the *Investigations* in the form of 'intentionality'. I am inclined to take §440 and §460 to refer obliquely to Russell's theory and to reject it.

Wittgenstein's remarks on machines (see pp. 33–4 and note 24 below) also express an explicit rejection of dispositional and causal accounts of meaning and following a rule.

[20] Actually such a crude definition is quite obviously inapplicable to functions that I can define but cannot compute by any algorithm. Granted Church's thesis, such functions abound. (See the remark on Turing machines in footnote 24 below.) However, Wittgenstein himself does not consider such functions when he develops his paradox. For symbols denoting such functions the question "What function do I mean by the symbol?" makes sense; but the usual Wittgensteinian paradox (any response, not just the one I give, accords with the rule) makes no sense, since there need be no response that I give if I have no procedure for computing values of the function. Nor does a dispositional account of what I mean make sense. – This is not the place to go into such matters: for Wittgenstein, it may be connected with his relations to finitism and intuitionism.

simply too large for my mind – or my brain – to grasp. When given such sums, I may shrug my shoulders for lack of comprehension; I may even, if the numbers involved are large enough, die of old age before the questioner completes his question. Let 'quaddition' be redefined so as to be a function which agrees with addition for all pairs of numbers small enough for me to have any disposition to add them, and let it diverge from addition thereafter (say, it is 5). Then, just as the sceptic previously proposed the hypothesis that I meant quaddition in the old sense, now he proposes the hypothesis that I meant quaddition in the new sense. A dispositional account will be impotent to refute him. As before, there are infinitely many candidates the sceptic can propose for the role of quaddition.

I have heard it suggested that the trouble arises solely from too crude a notion of disposition: *ceteris paribus*, I surely will respond with the sum of any two numbers when queried. And *ceteris paribus* notions of dispositions, not crude and literal notions, are the ones standardly used in philosophy and in science. Perhaps, but how should we flesh out the *ceteris paribus* clause? Perhaps as something like: if my brain had been stuffed with sufficient extra matter to grasp large enough numbers, and if it were given enough capacity to perform such a large addition, and if my life (in a healthy state) were prolonged enough, then given an addition problem involving two large numbers, *m* and *n*, I would respond with their sum, and not with the result according to some quus-like rule. But how can we have any confidence of this? How in the world can I tell what would happen if my brain were stuffed with extra brain matter, or if my life were prolonged by some magic elixir? Surely such speculation should be left to science fiction writers and futurologists. We have no idea what the results of such experiments would be. They might lead me to go insane, even to behave according to a quus-like rule. The outcome really is obviously indeterminate, failing further specification of these magic mind-expanding processes; and even with such specifications, it is highly speculative. But of course what the *ceteris paribus* clause really means is something like this: If I somehow were to be given the means to carry out my intentions with respect to numbers that presently are too long for me to add (or to grasp), and if I were to carry out these intentions, then if queried about '$m+n$' for some big m and n, I would respond with their sum (and not with their quum). Such a counterfactual conditional is true enough, but it is of no help against the sceptic. It presupposes a prior notion of my having an intention to mean one function rather than another by '$+$'. It is in virtue of a fact of this kind about me that the conditional is true. But of course the sceptic is challenging the existence of just such a fact; his challenge must be met by specifying its nature. Granted that I mean addition by '$+$', then of course if I were to act in accordance with my intentions, I would respond, given any pair of numbers to be combined by '$+$', with their sum; but equally, granted that I mean quaddition, if I were to act in accordance with my intentions, I would respond with the quum. One cannot favor one conditional rather than another without circularity.

Recapitulating briefly: if the dispositionalist attempts to define which function I meant as the function determined by the answer I am disposed to give for arbitrarily large arguments, he ignores the fact that my dispositions extend to only finitely many cases. If he tries to appeal to my responses under idealized conditions that overcome this finiteness, he will succeed only if the idealization includes a specification that I will still respond, under these idealized conditions, according to the infinite table of the function I actually meant. But then the circularity of the procedure is evident. The idealized dispositions are determinate only because it is already settled which function I meant.

The dispositionalist labors under yet another, equally potent, difficulty, which was foreshadowed above when I recalled Wittgenstein's remark that, if 'right' makes sense, it cannot be the case that whatever seems right to me is (by definition) right. Most of us have dispositions to make mistakes.[21] For example, when asked to add certain numbers some people forget to 'carry'. They are thus disposed, for these numbers, to give an answer differing from the usual addition table. Normally, we say that such people have made a *mistake*. That means, that for them as for us, '+' means addition, but for certain numbers they are not disposed to give the answer they *should* give, if they are to accord with the table of the function they actually *meant*. But the dispositionalist cannot say this. According to him, the function someone means is to be *read off* from his dispositions; it cannot be

[21] However, in the slogan quoted and in §202, Wittgenstein seems to be more concerned with the question, "Am I right in thinking that I am still applying the same rule?" than with the question "Is my application of the rule right?" Relatively few of us have the disposition – as far as I know – bizarrely to cease to apply a given rule if once we were applying it. Perhaps there is a corrosive substance present in my brain already (whose action will be 'triggered' if I am given a certain addition problem) that will lead me to forget how to add. I might, once this substance is secreted, start giving bizarre answers to addition problems – answers that conform to a quus-like rule, or to no discernible pattern at all. Even if I do think that I am following the same rule, in fact I am not.

Now, when I assert that I definitely mean addition by 'plus', am I making a *prediction* about my future behavior, asserting that there is no such corrosive acid? To put the matter differently: I assert that the present meaning I give to '+' determines values for arbitrarily large amounts. I do *not* predict that I will come out with these values, or even that I will use anything like the 'right' procedures to get them. A disposition to go berserk, to change the rule, etc., may be in me already, waiting to be triggered by the right stimulus. I make no assertion about such possibilities when I say that my use of the '+' sign determines values for every pair of arguments. Much less do I assert that the values I will come out with under these circumstances are, by definition, the values that accord with what is meant.

These possibilities, and the case mentioned above with '*', when I am disposed to respond even though I follow no rule from the beginning, should be borne in mind in addition to the garden-variety possibility of error mentioned in the text. Note that in the case of '*', it seems intuitively possible that I could be under the impression that I was following a rule even though I was following none – see the analogous case of reading on pp. 45–6 below, in reference to §166.

presupposed in advance which function is meant. In the present instance a certain unique function (call it 'skaddition') corresponds in its table exactly to the subject's dispositions, including his dispositions to make mistakes. (Waive the difficulty that the subject's dispositions are finite: suppose he has a disposition to respond to any pair of arguments.) So, where common sense holds that the subject means the same addition function as everyone else but systematically makes computational mistakes, the dispositionalist seems forced to hold that the subject makes no computational mistakes, but means a non-standard function ('skaddition') by '+'. Recall that the dispositionalist held that we would detect someone who meant quus by '+' *via* his disposition to respond with '5' for arguments ⩾57. In the same way, he will 'detect' that a quite ordinary, though fallible, subject means some non-standard function by '+'.

Once again, the difficulty cannot be surmounted by a *ceteris paribus* clause, by a clause excluding 'noise', or by a distinction between 'competence' and 'performance'. No doubt a disposition to give the true sum in response to each addition problem is part of my 'competence', if by this we mean simply that such an answer accords with the rule I intended, or if we mean that, if all my dispositions to make mistakes were removed, I would give the correct answer. (Again I waive the finiteness of my capacity.) But a disposition to make a mistake is simply a disposition to *give an answer other than the one that accords with the function I meant*. To presuppose this concept in the present discussion is of course viciously circular. If I meant addition, my 'erroneous' actual disposition is to be ignored; if I meant skaddition, it should not be. Nothing in the notion of my 'competence' as thus defined can possibly tell me which alternative to adopt.[22] Alternatively, we might try to specify

---

[22] Lest I be misunderstood, I hope it is clear that in saying this I do not myself reject Chomsky's competence–performance distinction. On the contrary, I personally find that the familiar arguments for the distinction (and for the attendant notion of grammatical rule) have great persuasive force. The present work is intended to expound my understanding of

the 'noise' to be ignored without presupposing a prior notion
of which function is meant. A little experimentation will
reveal the futility of such an effort. Recall that the subject has a

---

Wittgenstein's position, not my own; but I certainly do not mean,
exegetically, to assert that Wittgenstein himself would reject the distinction. But what *is* important here is that the notion of 'competence' is itself
not a dispositional notion. It is normative, not descriptive, in the sense
explained in the text.

The point is that our understanding of the notion of 'competence' is
dependent on our understanding of the idea of 'following a rule', as is
argued in the discussion above. Wittgenstein would reject the idea that
'competence' can be defined in terms of an idealized dispositional or
mechanical model, and used without circularity to explicate the notion of
following a rule. Only after the sceptical problem about rules has been
resolved can we *then* define 'competence' in terms of rule-following.
Although notions of 'competence' and 'performance' differ (at least)
from writer to writer, I see no reason why linguists need assume that
'competence' is defined prior to rule-following. Although the remarks in
the text warn against the use of the 'competence' notion as a solution to
our problem, in no way are they arguments against the notion itself.

Nevertheless, given the sceptical nature of Wittgenstein's solution to
his problem (as this solution is explained below), it is clear that if
Wittgenstein's standpoint is accepted, the notion of 'competence' will be
seen in a light radically different from the way it implicitly is seen in much
of the literature of linguistics. For *if* statements attributing rule-following
are neither to be regarded as stating facts, nor to be thought of as
explaining our behavior (see section 3 below), it would seem that the *use* of
the ideas of rules and of competence in linguistics needs serious
reconsideration, even if these notions are not rendered 'meaningless'.
(Depending on one's standpoint, one might view the tension revealed
here between modern linguistics and Wittgenstein's sceptical critique as
casting doubt on the linguistics, or on Wittgenstein's sceptical critique –
or both.) These questions would arise even if, as throughout the present
text, we deal with rules, like addition, that are stated explicitly. These
rules we think of ourselves as grasping consciously; in the absence of
Wittgenstein's sceptical arguments, we would see no problem in the
assumption that each particular answer we produce is justified by our
'grasp' of the rules. The problems are compounded if, as in linguistics,
the rules are thought of as tacit, to be reconstructed by the scientist and
inferred as an *explanation* of behavior. The matter deserves an extended
discussion elsewhere. (See also pp. 97 to 99 and n. 77 below.)

systematic disposition to forget to carry in certain circumstances: he tends to give a uniformly erroneous answer when well rested, in a pleasant environment free of clutter, etc. One cannot repair matters by urging that the subject would eventually respond with the right answer after correction by others. First, there are uneducable subjects who will persist in their error even after persistent correction. Second, what is meant by 'correction by others'? If it means rejection by others of 'wrong' answers (answers that do not accord with the rule the speaker means) and suggestion of the right answer (the answer that does accord), then again the account is circular. If random intervention is allowed (that is, the 'corrections' may be arbitrary, whether they are 'right' or 'wrong'), then, although educable subjects may be induced to correct their wrong answers, suggestible subjects may also be induced to replace their correct answers with erroneous ones. The amended dispositional statement will, then, provide no criterion for the function that is really meant.

The dispositional theory, as stated, assumes that which function I meant is determined by my dispositions to compute its values in particular cases. In fact, this is not so. Since dispositions cover only a finite segment of the total function and since they may deviate from its true values, two individuals may agree on their computations in particular cases even though they are actually computing different functions. Hence the dispositional view is not correct.

In discussions, I have sometimes heard a variant of the dispositional account. The argument goes as follows: the sceptic argues, in essence, that I am free to give any new answer to an addition problem, since I can always interpret my previous intentions appropriately. But how can this be? As Dummett put the objection: "A machine can follow this rule; whence does a human being gain a freedom of choice in this matter which a machine does not possess?"[23] The objection is

[23] M. A. E. Dummett, "Wittgenstein's Philosophy of Mathematics," *The Philosophical Review*, vol. 68 (1959), pp. 324–48, see p. 331; reprinted in George Pitcher (ed.), *Wittgenstein: The Philosophical Investigations* (Mac-

really a form of the dispositional account, for that account can be viewed as if it interpreted us as machines, whose output mechanically yields the correct result.

We can interpret the objector as arguing that the rule can be *embodied* in a machine that computes the relevant function. If I build such a machine, it will simply grind out the right answer, in any particular case, to any particular addition problem. The answer that the machine would give is, then, the answer that I intended.

The term 'machine' is here, as often elsewhere in philosophy, ambiguous. Few of us are in a position to build a machine or draw up a program to embody our intentions; and if a technician performs the task for me, the sceptic can ask legitimately whether the technician has performed his task correctly. Suppose, however, that I am fortunate enough to be such an expert that I have the technical facility required to embody my own intentions in a computing machine, and I state that the machine is *definitive* of my own intentions. Now the word 'machine' here may refer to any one of various things. It may refer to a machine *program* that I draw up, embodying my intentions as to the operation of the machine. Then exactly the same problems arise for the program as for the original symbol '+': the sceptic can feign to believe that the program, too, ought to be interpreted in a quus-like manner. To say that a program is not something that I wrote down on paper, but an abstract mathematical object, gets us no further. The problem then simply takes the form of the question: what program (in the sense of abstract mathematical object) corresponds to the 'program' I have written on paper (in accordance with the way I meant it)? ('Machine' often seems to mean a program in one of these senses: a Turing 'machine', for example, would be better called a 'Turing program'.) Finally, however, I may build a concrete machine, made of metal and

millan, 1966, pp. 420–47), see p. 428. The quoted objection need not necessarily be taken to express Dummett's own ultimate view of the matter.

gears (or transistors and wires), and declare that it embodies
the function I intend by '+': the values that it gives are the
values of the function I intend. However, there are several
problems with this. First, even if I say that the machine
embodies the function in this sense, I must do so in terms of
instructions (machine 'language', coding devices) that tell me
how to interpret the machine; further, I must declare explicitly
that the function always takes values as given, in accordance
with the chosen code, by the machine. But then the sceptic is
free to interpret all these instructions in a non-standard,
'quus-like' way. Waiving this problem, there are two others –
here is where the previous discussion of the dispositional view
comes in. I cannot really insist that the values of the function
are given by the machine. First, the machine is a finite object,
accepting only finitely many numbers as input and yielding
only finitely many as output – others are simply too big.
Indefinitely many programs extend the actual finite behavior
of the machine. Usually this is ignored because the designer of
the machine intended it to fulfill just one program, but in the
present context such an approach to the intentions of the
designer simply gives the sceptic his wedge to interpret in a
non-standard way. (Indeed, the appeal to the designer's
program makes the physical machine superfluous; only the
program is really relevant. The machine as physical object is of
value only if the intended function can somehow be read off
from the physical object alone.) Second, in practice it hardly is
likely that I really intend to entrust the values of a function to
the operation of a physical machine, even for that finite
portion of the function for which the machine can operate.
Actual machines can *malfunction*: through melting wires or
slipping gears they may give the wrong answer. How is it
determined when a malfunction occurs? By reference to the
program of the machine, as intended by its designer, not
simply by reference to the machine itself. Depending on the
intent of the designer, any particular phenomenon may or
may not count as a machine 'malfunction'. A programmer
with suitable intentions might even have intended to make use

of the fact that wires melt or gears slip, so that a machine that is 'malfunctioning' for me is behaving perfectly for him. Whether a machine ever malfunctions and, if so, when, is not a property of the machine itself as a physical object but is well defined only in terms of its program, as stipulated by its designer. Given the program, once again the physical object is superfluous for the purpose of determining what function is meant. Then, as before, the sceptic can concentrate his objections on the program. The last two criticisms of the use of the physical machine as a way out of scepticism – its finitude and the possibility of malfunction – obviously parallel two corresponding objections to the dispositional account.[24]

---

[24] Wittgenstein discusses machines explicitly in §§193–5. See the parallel discussion in *Remarks on the Foundations of Mathematics*, part I, §§118–30, especially §§119–26; see also, e.g., II [III], §87, and III [IV], §§48–9 there. The criticisms in the text of the dispositional analysis and of the use of machines to solve the problem are inspired by these sections. In particular, Wittgenstein himself draws the distinction between the machine as an abstract program ("der Maschine, als Symbol" §193) and the actual physical machine, which is subject to breakdown ("do we forget the possibility of their bending, breaking off, melting, and so on?" (§193)). The dispositional theory views the subject himself as a kind of machine, whose potential actions embody the function. So in this sense the dispositional theory and the idea of the machine-as-embodying-the-function are really one. Wittgenstein's attitude toward both is the same: they confuse the 'hardness of a rule' with the 'hardness of a material' (*RFM*, II [III], §87). On my interpretation, then, Wittgenstein agrees with his interlocutor (§194 and §195) that the sense in which all the values of the function are already present is not simply causal, although he disagrees with the idea that the future use is already present in some mysterious non-causal way.

Although, in an attempt to follow Wittgenstein, I have emphasized the distinction between concrete physical machines and their abstract programs in what I have written above, it might be instructive to look at the outcome when the limitation of machines is idealized as in the modern theory of automata. A finite automaton, as usually defined, has only finitely many states, receives only finitely many distinct inputs, and has only finitely many outputs, but it is idealized in two respects: it has no problem of malfunction, and its lifetime (without any decay or wearing out of its parts) is infinite. Such a machine can, in a sense, perform computations on arbitrarily large whole numbers. If it has notations for the single digits from zero through nine, inclusive, it can receive arbitrarily large positive whole numbers as inputs simply by being given their digits one by one. (We cannot do this, since our effective lifetimes are finite, and there is a minimum time needed for us to understand any single digit.) Such an automaton can add according to the usual algorithm in decimal notation (the digits for the numbers being added should be fed into the machine starting from the last digits of both summands and going backwards, as in the usual algorithm). However, it can be proved that, in the same ordinary decimal notation, such a machine cannot *multiply*. Any function computed by such a machine that purports to be multiplication will, for large enough arguments, exhibit 'quus-like' (or rather, 'quimes-like') properties at sufficiently large arguments. Even if we were idealized as finite automata, a dispositional theory would yield unacceptable results.

Suppose we idealized even further and considered a Turing machine which has a tape to use which is infinite in both directions. Such a machine has infinite extent at every moment, in addition to an infinite lifetime without malfunctions. Turing machines can multiply correctly, but it is well known that even here there are many functions we can define explicitly that can be computed by no such machine. A crude dispositional theory would attribute to us a non-standard interpretation (or no interpretation at all) for any such function. (See above, note 20.)

I have found that both the crude dispositional theory and the function-as-embodied-in-a-machine come up frequently when Wittgenstein's paradox is discussed. For this reason, and because of their close relation to Wittgenstein's text, I have expounded these theories, though sometimes I have wondered whether the discussion of them is excessively long. On the other hand, I have resisted the temptation to discuss 'functionalism' explicitly, even though various forms of it have been so attractive to so many of the best recent writers that it has almost become the received philosophy of mind in the USA. Especially I have feared that some readers of the discussion in the text will think that 'functionalism' is precisely the way to modify the crude dispositional theory so as to meet the criticisms (especially those that rely on the circularity of *ceteris paribus* clauses). (I report, however, that thus far I have not run into such reactions in practice.) I cannot discuss functionalism at length here without straying from the main point. But I offer a brief hint. Functionalists are fond of comparing psychological states to the abstract states of a (Turing) machine, though some are cognizant of certain limitations of the comparison. All regard psychology as given by a set of causal connections, analogous to the *causal* operation of a machine. But then the remarks of the text stand here as well: any concrete physical object can be viewed as an imperfect realization of many machine programs. Taking a human organism as a concrete object, what is to tell

The moral of the present discussion of the dispositional account may be relevant to other areas of concern to philosophers beyond the immediate point at issue. Suppose I do mean addition by '+'. What is the relation of this supposition to the question how I will respond to the problem '68+57'? The dispositionalist gives a *descriptive* account of this relation: if '+' meant addition, then I will answer '125'. But this is not the proper account of the relation, which is *normative*, not descriptive. The point is *not* that, if I meant addition by '+', I will answer '125', but that, if I intend to accord with my past meaning of '+', I *should* answer '125'. Computational error, finiteness of my capacity, and other disturbing factors may lead me not to be *disposed* to respond as I *should*, but if so, I have not acted in accordance with my intentions. The relation of meaning and intention to future action is *normative*, not *descriptive*.

In the beginning of our discussion of the dispositional analysis, we suggested that it had a certain air of irrelevance with respect to a significant aspect of the sceptical problem – that the fact that the sceptic can maintain the hypothesis that I meant quus shows that I had no *justification* for answering '125' rather than '5'. How does the dispositional analysis even appear to touch this problem? Our conclusion in the previous paragraph shows that in some sense, after giving a number of more specific criticisms of the dispositional theory, we have returned full circle to our original intuition. Precisely the fact that our answer to the question of which function I meant is *justificatory* of my present response is ignored in the dispositional account and leads to all its difficulties.

I shall leave the dispositional view. Perhaps I have already belabored it too much. Let us repudiate briefly another

---

us *which* program he should be regarded as instantiating? In particular, does he compute 'plus' or 'quus'? If the remarks on machines in my own (and Wittgenstein's) text are understood, I think it will emerge that as far as the present problem is concerned, Wittgenstein would regard his remarks on machines as applicable to 'functionalism' as well.

I hope to elaborate on these remarks elsewhere.

suggestion. Let no one – under the influence of too much philosophy of science – suggest that the hypothesis that I meant plus is to be preferred as the *simplest* hypothesis. I will not here argue that simplicity is relative, or that it is hard to define, or that a Martian might find the quus function simpler than the plus function. Such replies may have considerable merit, but the real trouble with the appeal to simplicity is more basic. Such an appeal must be based either on a misunderstanding of the sceptical problem, or of the role of simplicity considerations, or both. Recall that the sceptical problem was not merely epistemic. The sceptic argues that there is no fact as to what I meant, whether plus or quus. Now simplicity considerations can help us decide between competing hypotheses, but they obviously can never tell us what the competing hypotheses are. If we do not understand what two hypotheses *state*, what does it mean to say that one is 'more probable' because it is 'simpler'? If the two competing hypotheses are not genuine hypotheses, not assertions of genuine matters of fact, no 'simplicity' considerations will make them so.

Suppose there are two conflicting hypotheses about electrons, both confirmed by the experimental data. If our own view of statements about electrons is 'realist' and not 'instrumentalist', we will view these assertions as making factual assertions about some 'reality' about electrons. God, or some appropriate being who could 'see' the facts about electrons directly, would have no need for experimental evidence or simplicity considerations to decide between hypotheses. We, who lack such capacities, must rely on indirect evidence, from the effects of the electrons on the behavior of gross objects, to decide between the hypotheses. If two competing hypotheses are indistinguishable as far as their effects on gross objects are concerned, then *we* must fall back on simplicity considerations to decide between them. A being – not ourselves – who could 'see' the facts about electrons 'directly' would have no need to invoke simplicity considerations, nor to rely on indirect evidence to decide between the hypotheses; he would 'directly perceive' the relevant facts that make one hypothesis true rather than another. To say this is simply to repeat, in colorful terminology, the assertion that the two hypotheses do state genuinely different matters of fact.

Now Wittgenstein's sceptic argues that he knows of no fact about an individual that could constitute his state of meaning plus rather than quus. Against *this* claim simplicity considerations are irrelevant. Simplicity considerations would have been relevant against a sceptic who argued that the indirectness of our access to the facts of meaning and intention *prevents us ever from knowing* whether we mean plus or quus. But such merely epistemological scepticism is *not* in question. The sceptic does not argue that our own limitations of access to the facts prevent us from knowing something hidden. He claims that an omniscient being, with access to *all* available facts, still would not find any fact that differentiates between the plus and the quus hypotheses. Such an omniscient being would have neither need nor use for simplicity considerations.[25]

[25] A different use of 'simplicity', not that by which we evaluate competing theories, might suggest itself with respect to the discussion of machines above. There I remarked that a concrete physical machine, considered as an object without reference to a designer, may (approximately) instantiate any number of programs that (approximately, allowing for some 'malfunctioning') extend its actual finite behavior. If the physical machine was not designed but, so to speak, 'fell from the sky', there can be no fact of the matter as to which program it 'really' instantiates, hence no 'simplest hypothesis' about this non-existent fact.

Nevertheless, given a physical machine, one might ask what is the *simplest program* that the physical machine approximates. To do this one would have to find a measure of the simplicity of programs, a measure of the trade-off of the simplicity of the program with the degree to which the concrete machine fails to conform to it (malfunctions), and so on. I who am no expert, nor even an amateur, am unaware that this problem has been considered by theoretical computer scientists. Whether or not it has been considered, intuition suggests that something might be made of it, though it would not be trivial to find simplicity measures that give intuitively satisfying results.

I doubt that any of this would illuminate Wittgenstein's sceptical paradox. One might try, say, to define the function I meant as the one that, according to the simplicity measure, followed the simplest program

The idea that we lack 'direct' access to the facts whether we
mean plus or quus is bizarre in any case. Do I not know,
directly, and with a fair degree of certainty, that I mean plus?
Recall that a fact as to what I mean now is supposed to *justify*
my future actions, to make them *inevitable* if I wish to use
words with the same meaning with which I used them before.
This was our fundamental requirement on a fact as to what I
meant. No 'hypothetical' state could satisfy such a requirement: If I can only form hypotheses as to whether I now mean
plus or quus, if the truth of the matter is buried deep in my
unconscious and can only be posited as a tentative hypothesis,
then in the future I can only proceed hestitatingly and
hypothetically, *conjecturing* that I probably ought to answer
'68 + 57' with '125' rather than '5'. Obviously, this is not an
accurate account of the matter. There may be some facts about
me to which my access is indirect, and about which I must
form tentative hypotheses: but surely the fact as to what I
mean by 'plus' is not one of them! To say that it is, is already to
take a big step in the direction of scepticism. Remember that I
immediately and unhesitatingly calculate '68 + 57' as I do, and
the meaning I assign to '+' is supposed to *justify* this
procedure. I do not form tentative hypotheses, wondering
what I should do if one hypothesis or another were true.

Now the reference, in our exposition, to what an omniscient being could or would know is merely a dramatic device.
When the sceptic denies that even God, who knows all the

----

approximately compatible with my physical structure. Suppose brain
physiologists found – to their surprise – that actually such a simplicity
measure led to a program that did not compute addition for the '+'
function, but some other function. Would this show that I did not mean
addition by '+'? Yet, in the absence of detailed knowledge of the brain
(and the hypothetical simplicity measure), the physiological discovery in
question is by no means inconceivable. The justificatory aspect of the
sceptic's problem is even more obviously remote from any such
simplicity measure. I do not justify my choice of '125' rather than '5' as an
answer to '68 + 57' by citing a hypothetical simplicity measure of the type
mentioned. (I hope to elaborate on this in the projected work on
functionalism mentioned in note 24 above.)

facts, could know whether I meant plus or quus, he is simply giving colorful expression to his denial that there is any fact of the matter as to which I meant. Perhaps if we remove the metaphor we may do better. The metaphor, perhaps, may seduce us towards scepticism by encouraging us to look for a reduction of the notions of meaning and intention to something else. Why not argue that "meaning addition by 'plus'" denotes an irreducible experience, with its own special *quale*, known directly to each of us by introspection? (Headaches, tickles, nausea are examples of inner states with such *qualia*.)[26] Perhaps the "decisive move in the conjuring trick" has been made when the sceptic notes that I have performed only finitely many additions and challenges me, in the light of *this* fact, to adduce some fact that 'shows' that I did not mean quus. Maybe I appear to be unable to reply just because the experience of meaning addition by 'plus' is as unique and irreducible as that of seeing yellow or feeling a headache, while the sceptic's challenge invites me to look for another fact or experience to which this can be reduced.

I referred to an *introspectible* experience because, since each of us knows immediately and with fair certainty that he means addition by 'plus', presumably the view in question assumes we know this in the same way we know that we have headaches – by attending to the 'qualitative' character of our own experiences. Presumably the experience of *meaning addition* has its own irreducible quality, as does that of feeling a headache. The fact that I mean addition by 'plus' is to be identified with my possession of an experience of this quality.

Once again, as in the case of the dispositional account, the proffered theory seems to be off target as an answer to the original challenge of the sceptic. The sceptic wanted to know why I was so sure that I ought to say '125', when asked about '68 + 57'. I had never thought of this particular addition before: is not an interpretation of the '+' sign as quus compatible with everything I thought? Well, suppose I do in fact feel a certain

[26] It is well known that this type of view is characteristic of Hume's philosophy. See note 51 below.

headache with a very special quality whenever I think of the
'+' sign. How on earth would this headache help me figure
out whether I ought to answer '125' or '5' when asked about
'68 + 57'? If I think the headache indicates that I ought to say
'125', would there be anything about it to refute a sceptic's
contention that, on the contrary, it indicates that I should say
'5'? The idea that each of my inner states – including,
presumably, meaning what I do by 'plus' – has its special
discernible quality like a headache, a tickle, or the experience
of a blue after-image, is indeed one of the cornerstones of
classical empiricism. Cornerstone it may be, but it is very hard
to see how the alleged introspectible *quale* could be relevant to
the problem at hand.

Similar remarks apply even to those cases where the classical
empiricist picture might seem to have a greater plausibility.
This picture suggested that association of an image with a
word (paradigmatically a visual one) determined its meaning.
For example (§139), a drawing of a cube comes to my mind
whenever I hear or say the word 'cube'. It should be obvious
that this need not be the case. Many of us use words such as
'cube' even though no such drawing or image comes to mind.
Let us suppose, however, for the moment that one does. 'In
what sense can this picture fit or fail to fit a use of the word
"cube"? – Perhaps you say: "It's quite simple; – if that picture
comes to me and I point to a triangular prism for instance, and
say it's a cube, then this use of the word doesn't fit the
picture." But doesn't it fit? I have purposely so chosen the
example that it is quite easy to imagine a *method of projection*
according to which the picture does fit after all. The picture of
the cube did indeed *suggest* a certain use to us, but it was
possible for me to use it differently.' The sceptic could suggest
that the image be used in non-standard ways. 'Suppose,
however, that not merely the picture of the cube, but also the
method of projection comes before our mind? – How am I to
imagine this? – Perhaps I see before me a schema showing the
method of projection: say a picture of two cubes connected by
lines of projection. – But does this really get me any further?

Can't I now imagine different applications of this schema too?' (§141). Once again, a rule for interpreting a rule. No internal impression, with a *quale*, could possibly tell me in itself how it is to be applied in future cases. Nor can any pile up of such impressions, thought of as rules for interpreting rules, do the job.[27] The answer to the sceptic's problem, "What tells me how I am to apply a given rule in a new case?", must come from something outside any images or 'qualitative' mental states. This is obvious, in the case of 'plus' – it is clear enough that no internal state such as a headache, a tickle, an image, could do the job. (Obviously I do not have an image of the infinite table of the 'plus' function in my mind. Some such image would be the only candidate that even has surface plausibility as a device for telling me how to apply 'plus'.) It may be less obvious in other cases, such as 'cube', but in fact it is also true of such cases as well.

So: If there were a special experience of 'meaning' addition by 'plus', analogous to a headache, it would not have the properties that a state of meaning addition by 'plus' ought to have – it would not tell me what to do in new cases. In fact, however, Wittgenstein extensively argues in addition that the supposed unique special experience of meaning (addition by 'plus', etc.) does not exist. His investigation here is an introspective one, designed to show that the supposed unique experience is a chimera. Of all the replies to the sceptic he combats, the view of meaning as an introspectible experience is probably the most natural and fundamental. But for the present day audience I dealt with it neither first nor at greatest length, for, though the Humean picture of an irreducible 'impression' corresponding to each psychological state or event has tempted many in the past, it tempts relatively few today. In fact, if in the past it was too readily and simplistically assumed, at present its force is – at least in my personal opinion – probably too *little* felt. There are several reasons for this. One is that, in this instance, Wittgenstein's critique of alternative

---

[27] The remarks above, p. 20, on the use of an image, or even a physical sample, of green make the same point.

views has been relatively well received and absorbed. And related writers – such as Ryle – have reinforced the critique of the Cartesian and Humean pictures. Another reason – unattractive to the present writer – has been the popularity of materialistic-behavioristic views that ignore the problem of felt qualities of mental states altogether, or at least attempt to analyze all such states away in broadly behavioristic terms.[28]

It is important to repeat in the present connection what I have said above: Wittgenstein does not base his considerations on any behavioristic *premise* that dismisses the 'inner'. On the contrary, much of his argumentation consists in detailed introspective considerations. Careful consideration of our inner lives, he argues, will show that there is no special inner experience of 'meaning' of the kind supposed by his opponent. The case is specifically in *contrast* with feeling a pain, seeing red, and the like.

It takes relatively little introspective acuteness to realize the dubiousness of the attribution of a special qualitative character to the 'experience' of meaning addition by 'plus'. Attend to what happened when I first learned to add. First, there may or may not have been a specifiable time, probably in my childhood, at which I suddenly felt (*Eureka!*) that I had grasped the rule for addition. If there was not, it is very hard to see in what the suppositious special experience of my learning to add consisted. Even if there was a particular time at which I could have shouted "*Eureka!*" – surely the exceptional case – in what did the attendant experience consist? Probably consideration of a few particular cases and a thought – "Now I've got it!" – or the like. Could just *this* be the content of an experience of 'meaning addition'? How would it have been different if I had

---

[28] Although there are clear classical senses of behaviorism in which such current philosophies of mind as 'functionalism' are not behaviorist, nevertheless, speaking for myself, I find much contemporary 'functionalism' (especially those versions that attempt to give 'functional' *analyses* of mental terms) are far too behavioristic for my own taste. It would require an extensive digression to go into the matter further here.

meant quus? Suppose I perform a particular addition now, say '5 + 7'. Is there any special quality to the experience? Would it have been different if I had been trained in, and performed, the corresponding quaddition? How different indeed would the *experience* have been if I had performed the corresponding multiplication ('5 × 7'), other than that I would have responded automatically with a different answer? (Try the experiment yourself.)

Wittgenstein returns to points like these repeatedly throughout *Philosophical Investigations.* In the sections where he discusses his sceptical paradox (§§137–242), after a general consideration of the alleged introspectible process of understanding, he considers the issue in connection with the special case of *reading* (§§156–78). By 'reading' Wittgenstein means reading out loud what is written or printed and similar activities: he is not concerned with understanding what is written. I myself, like many of my coreligionists, first learned to 'read' Hebrew in this sense before I could understand more than a few words of the language. Reading in this sense is a simple case of 'following a rule'. Wittgenstein points out that a beginner, who reads by laboriously spelling words out, may have an introspectible experience when he really reads, as opposed to pretending to 'read' a passage he has actually memorized in advance; but an experienced reader simply calls the words out and is aware of no special conscious experience of 'deriving' the words from the page. The experienced reader may 'feel' nothing different when he reads from what the beginner feels, or does not feel, when he pretends. And suppose a teacher is teaching a number of beginners to read. Some pretend, others occasionally get it right by accident, others have already learned to read. When has someone passed into the latter class? In general, there will not be an identifiable moment when this has happened: the teacher will judge of a given pupil that he has 'learned to read' if he passes tests for reading often enough. There may or may not be an identifiable moment when the pupil first *felt,* "Now I am reading!" but the presence of such an experience is neither a necessary nor a sufficient condition for the teacher to judge of him that he is reading.

Again (§160), someone may, under the influence of a drug, or in a dream, be presented with a made-up 'alphabet' and utter certain words, with all the characteristic 'feeling' of reading, to the extent that such a 'feeling' exists at all. If, after the drug wears off (or he wakes up), he himself thinks he was uttering words at random with no real connection with the script, should we really say he was reading? Or, on the other hand, what if the drug leads him to read fluently from a genuine text, but with the 'sensation' of reciting something learned by heart? Wasn't he still reading?

It is by examples like these – *Philosophical Investigations* contains a wealth of examples and mental thought experiments beyond what I have summarized – that Wittgenstein argues that the supposed special 'experiences' associated with rule following are chimerical.[29] As I said, my own discussion

---

[29] The point should not be overstated. Although Wittgenstein does deny that there is any particular 'qualitative' experience like a headache, present when and only when we use a word with a certain meaning (or read, or understand, etc.), he does acknowledge a certain 'feel' to our meaningful use of a word that may under certain circumstances be lost. Many have had a fairly common experience: by repeating a word or phrase again and again, one may be able to deprive it of its normal 'life', so that it comes to sound strange and foreign, even though one is still able to utter it under the right circumstances. Here there is a special feeling of foreignness in a particular case. Could there be someone who always used words like a mechanism, without any 'feeling' of a distinction between this mechanistic type of use and the normal case? Wittgenstein is concerned with these matters in the second part of the *Investigations*, in connection with his discussion of 'seeing as' (section xi, pp. 193–229). Consider especially his remarks on 'aspect blindness', pp. 213–14, and the relation of 'seeing an aspect' to 'experiencing the meaning of a word', p. 214. (See his examples on p. 214: "What would you be missing . . . if you did not feel that a word lost its meaning and became a mere sound if it was repeated ten times over? . . . Suppose I had agreed on a code with someone; "tower" means bank. I tell him "Now go to the tower" – he understands me and acts accordingly, but he feels the word "tower" to be strange in this use, it

has not yet 'taken on' the meaning." He gives many examples on
pp. 213–18.)

Compare (as Wittgenstein does) the feeling of meaning a word as
such-and-such (think of 'till' now as a verb, now as a noun, etc.), with the
idea of visual aspects discussed at length in section xi of the second part of
the *Investigations*. We can see the duck-rabbit (p. 194) now as a rabbit,
now as a duck; we can see the Necker cube, now with one face forward,
now with another; we can see a cube drawing (p. 193) as a box, a wire
frame, etc. How, if at all, does our visual experience change? The
experience is much more elusive than is anything like the feeling of a
headache, the hearing of a sound, the visual experience of a blue patch.
The corresponding 'aspects' of meaning would seem to be introspectively
even more elusive.

Similarly, although some of the passages in §§156–78 seem to debunk
the idea of a conscious special experience of 'being guided' (when
reading) altogether, it seems wrong to think of it as totally dismissed. For
example, in §160, Wittgenstein speaks both of the 'sensation of saying
something he has learnt by heart' and of the 'sensation of reading', though
the point of the paragraph is that the presence or absence of such
sensations is not what constitutes the distinction between reading, saying
something by heart, and yet something else. To some extent, I think
Wittgenstein's discussion may have a certain ambivalence. Nevertheless,
some relevant points made are these: (i) Whatever an 'experience of being
guided' (in reading) may be, it is not something with a gross and
introspectible qualitative character, like a headache (contrary to Hume).
(ii) In particular cases of reading, we may feel definite and introspectible
experiences, but these are different and distinct experiences, peculiar to
each individual case, not a single experience present in all cases. (In the
same way, Wittgenstein speaks of various introspectible 'mental processes' that *in particular circumstances* occur when I understand a word – see
§§151–5, but none of these *is* the 'process' of understanding, indeed
understanding is not a 'mental process' – see pp. 49–51 below. The
discussion of reading, which follows §§151–5 immediately, is meant to
illustrate these points. (iii) Perhaps most important, whatever the elusive
feeling of being guided may be, its presence or absence is not constitutive
of whether I am reading or not. See, for example, the cases mentioned
above in the text, of the pupil learning to read and of the person under the
influence of a drug.

Rush Rhees, in his preface to *The Blue and Brown Books* (Basil
Blackwell, Oxford and Harper and Brothers, New York, 1958,
xiv+185 pp.) emphasizes (see pp. xii–xiv) the problem created for
Wittgenstein by 'meaning blindness', and he emphasizes that the
discussion of 'seeing something as something' in section xi of the second

can be brief because this particular Wittgensteinian lesson has been relatively well learned, perhaps too well learned. But some points should be noted. First, to repeat, the method of the investigation, and of the thought-experiments is deeply introspective: it is exactly the kind of investigation a strict psychological behaviorist would *prohibit*.[30] Second, although Wittgenstein does conclude that behavior, and dispositions to behavior, lead us to *say* of a person that he is reading, or adding, or whatever, this should not, in my opinion, be misconstrued as an endorsement of the dispositional theory: he does not say that reading or adding *is* a certain disposition to behavior.[31]

part of *Philosophical Investigations* is motivated by an attempt to deal with the elusive question. Earlier portions of the *Investigations* repudiate traditional pictures of internal, qualitative states of meaning and understanding; but later Wittgenstein seems, as Rhees says, to be worried that he may be in danger of replacing the classical picture by an overly mechanistic one, though certainly he still repudiates any idea that a certain qualitative experience *is* what constitutes my using words with a certain meaning. Could there be a 'meaning blind' person who operated with words just as we do? If so, would we say that he is as much in command of the language as we? The 'official' answer to the second question, as given in our main text, is 'yes'; but perhaps the answer should be, "Say what you want, as long as you know the facts." It is not clear that the problem is entirely resolved. Note that here, too, the discussion is introspective, based on an investigation of our own phenomenal experience. It is not the kind of investigation that would be undertaken by a behaviorist. No doubt the matter deserves a careful and extended treatment.

[30] §314 says: "It shows a fundamental misunderstanding, if I am inclined to study the headache I have now in order to get clear about the fundamental philosophical problem of sensation." If this remark is to be consistent with Wittgenstein's frequent practice as outlined in the text above and note 29, it *cannot* be read as *generally* condemning the philosophical use of introspective reflections on the phenomenology of our experience.

[31] I should not deny that Wittgenstein has important affinities to behaviorism (as to finitism — see pp. 105–7 below). Such a famous slogan as "My attitude towards him is an attitude towards a soul (*Seele*). I am not of the *opinion* that he has a soul" (p. 178) sounds much too behavioristic for me. I personally would like to think that anyone who does not think of me as conscious is wrong about the facts, not simply 'unfortunate', or 'evil', or

Wittgenstein's conviction of the contrast between states of understanding, reading and the like, and 'genuine', introspectible mental states or processes is so strong that it leads him – who is often regarded as a (or the) father of 'ordinary language philosophy', and who emphasizes the importance of respect for the way language is actually used – into some curious remarks about ordinary usage. Consider §154: "In the sense in which there are processes (including mental processes) which are characteristic of understanding, understanding is not a mental process. (A pain's growing more and less; the hearing of a tune or sentence: these are mental processes.)" Or again, at the bottom of p. 59, "'Understanding a word': a state. But a *mental* state? – Depression, excitement, pain, are called mental states. Carry out a grammatical investigation . . ." The terms 'mental state' and 'mental process' have a somewhat theoretical flavor, and I am not sure how firmly one can speak of their 'ordinary' use. However, my own linguistic intuitions do not entirely agree with Wittgenstein's remarks.[32] Coming to understand, or learning, seems to me to

___

even 'monstrous' or 'inhuman', in his 'attitude' (whatever that might mean).

    (If '*Seele*' is translated as 'soul', it might be thought that the 'attitude' (*Einstellung*') to which Wittgenstein refers has special religious connotations, or associations with Greek metaphysics and the accompanying philosophical tradition. But it is clear from the entire passage that the issue relates simply to the difference between my 'attitude' toward a conscious being and toward an automaton, even though one of the paragraphs refers specifically to the religious doctrine of the immortality of the soul ('*Seele*'). Perhaps in some respects 'mind' might be a less misleading translation of '*Seele*' in the sentence quoted above, since for the contemporary English speaking philosophical reader it is somewhat less loaded with special philosophical and religious connotations. I feel that this may be so even if 'soul' captures the flavor of the German '*Seele*' better than 'mind'. Anscombe translates '*Seele*' and its derivatives sometimes as 'soul', sometimes as 'mind', depending on the context. The problem really seems to be that German has only '*Seele*' and '*Geist*' to do duty where an English speaking philosopher would use 'mind'. See also the postscript below, note 11.

[32] These are my intuitions in English. I have no idea whether any differences

be a 'mental process' if anything is. A pain's growing more
and less, and especially the hearing of a tune or sentence, are
probably not ordinarily thought of as 'mental' processes at all.
Although depression and anxiety would ordinarily be called
'mental' states, pain (if genuine physical pain is meant) is
probably *not* a 'mental' state. ("It's all in your mind" means
that no genuine physical pain is present.) But Wittgenstein's
concern is not really with usage but with a philosophical
terminology. 'Mental states' and 'mental processes' are those
introspectible 'inner' contents that I can find in my mind, or
that God could find if he looked into my mind.[33] Such

---

with the German ('*seelischer Vorgang*' and '*seelischer Zustand*'), in nuance or
usage, affect the matter.

[33] Or so it would seem from the passages quoted. But the denial that
understanding is a 'mental process' in §154 is preceded by the weaker
remark, "Try not to think of understanding as a 'mental process' at all –
for that is the expression which confuses you." In itself, this seems to
say that thinking of understanding as a 'mental process' leads to misleading philosophical pictures, but not necessarily that it is wrong. See
also §§305–6: ' "But you surely cannot deny that, for example, in remembering, an inner process takes place."—What gives the impression
that we want to deny anything? . . . What we deny is that the picture of
the inner process gives us the correct use of the word "to remember"
. . . Why should I deny that there is a mental process? But "There has
just taken place in me the mental process of remembering . . ." means
nothing more than: "I have just remembered . . ." To deny the mental
process would mean to deny the remembering; to deny that anyone ever
remembers anything.' *This* passage gives the impression that *of course*
remembering is a 'mental process' if anything is, but that this ordinary
terminology is philosophically misleading. (The German here is
'*geistiger Vorgang*' while in the earlier passages it was '*seelischer Vorgang*'
(§154) and '*seelischer Zustand*' (p. 59), but as far as I can see, this has no
significance beyond stylistic variation. It is possible that the fact that
Wittgenstein speaks here of remembering, while earlier he had spoken
of understanding, is significant, but even this seems to me to be unlikely.
Note that in §154, the genuine 'mental processes' are a pain's growing
more or less, the hearing of a tune or sentence – processes with an
'introspectible quality' in the sense we have used the phrase. For Wittgenstein remembering is not a process like these, even though, as in the
case of understanding in §154, there may be processes with introspec-

phenomena, inasmuch as they are introspectible, 'qualitative' states of the mind, are not subject to immediate sceptical challenge of the present type. Understanding is not one of these.

Of course the falsity of the 'unique introspectible state' view of meaning plus must have been implicit from the start of the problem. If there really were an introspectible state, like a headache, of meaning addition by 'plus' (and if it really could have the justificatory role such a state ought to have), it would have stared one in the face and would have robbed the sceptic's challenge of any appeal. But given the force of this challenge, the need philosophers have felt to posit such a state and the loss we incur when we are robbed of it should be apparent. Perhaps we may try to recoup, by arguing that meaning addition by 'plus' is a state even more *sui generis* than we have argued before. Perhaps it is simply a primitive state, not to be assimilated to sensations or headaches or any 'qualitative' states, nor to be assimilated to dispositions, but a state of a unique kind of its own.

Such a move may in a sense be irrefutable, and if it is taken in an appropriate way Wittgenstein may even accept it. But it seems desperate: it leaves the nature of this postulated primitive state – the primitive state of 'meaning addition by "plus"' – completely mysterious. It is not supposed to be an introspectible state, yet we supposedly are aware of it with some fair degree of certainty whenever it occurs. For how else can each of us be confident that he *does*, at present, mean addition by 'plus'? Even more important is the logical difficulty implicit in Wittgenstein's sceptical argument. I think that Wittgenstein argues, not merely as we have said hitherto, that introspection shows that the alleged 'qualitative' state of understanding is a

---

tible qualities that take place when we remember. Assuming that the examples given in §154 are meant to be typical 'mental processes', the examples would be very misleading unless remembering were taken not to be a 'mental process' in the sense of §154. Remembering, like understanding, is an 'intentional' state (see note 19 above) subject to Wittgenstein's sceptical problem.) See also the discussion of 'incorporeal processes' in §339.)

chimera, but also that it is logically impossible (or at least that
there is a considerable logical difficulty) for there to be a state
of 'meaning addition by "plus"' at all.

Such a state would have to be a finite object, contained in
our finite minds.[34] It does not consist in my explicitly thinking
of each case of the addition table, nor even of my encoding
each separate case in the brain: we lack the capacity for that.
Yet (§195) "in a *queer* way" each such case already is "in some
sense present". (Before we hear Wittgenstein's sceptical
argument, we surely suppose – unreflectively – that something like this is indeed the case. Even now I have a strong
inclination to think this somehow must be right.) What can
that sense be? Can we conceive of a finite state which *could* not
be interpreted in a quus-like way? How could that be? The
proposal I am now discussing brushes such questions under
the rug, since the nature of the supposed 'state' is left

---

[34] We have stressed that I think of only finitely many cases of the addition
table. Anyone who claims to have thought of infinitely many cases of the
table is a liar. (Some philosophers – probably Wittgenstein – go so far as
to say that they see a conceptual incoherence in the supposition that
anyone thought of infinitely many such cases. We need not discuss the
merits of this strong view here as long as we acknowledge the weaker
claim that as a matter of fact each of us thinks of only finitely many cases.)
It is worth noting, however, that although it is useful, following
Wittgenstein himself, to *begin* the presentation of the puzzle with the
observation that I have thought of only finitely many cases, it appears that
in principle this particular ladder can be kicked away. Suppose that I had
explicitly thought of *all* cases of the addition table. How can this help me
answer the question '68+57'? Well, looking back over my own mental
records, I find that I gave myself explicit directions. "If you are ever asked
about '68+57', reply '125'!" Can't the sceptic say that these directions,
too, are to be interpreted in a non-standard way? (See *Remarks on the
Foundations of Mathematics*, I, §3: "If I know it *in advance*, what use is this
knowledge to me later on? I mean: how do I know what to do with this
earlier knowledge when the step is actually taken?") It would appear that,
if finiteness is relevant, it comes more crucially in the fact that
"justifications must come to an end somewhere" than in the fact that I
think of only finitely many cases of the addition table, even though
Wittgenstein stresses both facts. Either fact can be used to develop the
sceptical paradox; both are important.

mysterious. "But" – to quote the protest in §195 more fully – "I don't mean that what I do now (in grasping a sense) determines the future use *causally* and as a matter of experience, but that in a *queer* way, the use itself is in some sense present." A causal determination is the kind of analysis supposed by the dispositional theorist, and we have already seen that that is to be rejected. Presumably the relation now in question grounds some entailment roughly like: "If I now mean addition by 'plus'; then, if I remember this meaning in the future and wish to accord with what I meant, and do not miscalculate, then when asked for '68+57', I will respond '125'." If Hume is right, of course, no past state of my mind can entail that I will give any particular response in the future. But that I meant 125 in the past does not itself entail this; I must remember what I meant, and so on. Nevertheless it remains mysterious exactly how the existence of *any* finite past state of my mind could entail that, if I wish to accord with it, and remember the state, and do not miscalculate, I must give a determinate answer to an arbitrarily large addition problem.[35]

Mathematical realists, or 'Platonists', have emphasized the non-mental nature of mathematical entities. The addition function is not in any particular mind, nor is it the common property of all minds. It has an independent, 'objective', existence. There is then no problem – as far as the present considerations go – as to how the addition function (taken, say, as a set of triples)[36] contains within it all its instances, such as the triple (68, 57, 125). This simply is in the nature of the mathematical object in question, and it may well be an infinite

[35] See p. 218: "Meaning it is not a process which accompanies a word. For no process could have the consequences of meaning." This aphorism makes the general point sketched in the text. No process can entail what meaning entails. In particular, no process could entail the rough conditional stated above. See the discussion below, pp. 93–4, of Wittgenstein's view of these conditionals.

[36] Of course Frege would not accept the identification of a function with a set of triples. Such an identification violates his conception of functions as 'unsaturated'. Although this complication is very important for Frege's philosophy, it can be ignored for the purposes of the present presentation.

object. The proof that the addition function contains such a triple as (68, 57, 125) belongs to mathematics and has nothing to do with meaning or intention.

Frege's analysis of the usage of the plus sign by an individual posits the following four elements: (a) the addition function, an 'objective' mathematical entity; (b) the addition sign '+', a linguistic entity; (c) the 'sense' of this sign, an 'objective' abstract entity like the function; (d) an idea in the individual's mind associated with the sign. The idea is a 'subjective' mental entity, private to each individual and different in different minds. The 'sense', in contrast, is the same for all individuals who use '+' in the standard way. Each such individual grasps this sense by virtue of having an appropriate idea in his mind. The 'sense' in turn *determines* the addition function as the *referent* of the '+' sign.

There is again no special problem, for this position, as to the relation between the sense and the referent it determines. It simply is in the nature of a sense to determine a referent. But ultimately the sceptical problem cannot be evaded, and it arises precisely in the question how the existence in my mind of any mental entity or idea can *constitute* 'grasping' any particular sense rather than another. The idea in my mind is a finite object: can it not be interpreted as determining a quus function, rather than a plus function? Of course there may be another idea in my mind, which is supposed to constitute its act of *assigning* a particular interpretation to the first idea; but then the problem obviously arises again at this new level. (A rule for interpreting a rule again.) And so on. For Wittgenstein, Platonism is largely an unhelpful evasion of the problem of how our finite minds can give rules that are supposed to apply to an infinity of cases. Platonic objects may be self-interpreting, or rather, they may need no interpretation; but ultimately there must be some mental entity involved that raises the sceptical problem. (This brief discussion of Platonism is meant for those interested in the issue. If it is so brief that you find it obscure, ignore it.)

3

The Solution and the 'Private Language' Argument

The sceptical argument, then, remains unanswered. There can be no such thing as meaning anything by any word. Each new application we make is a leap in the dark; any present intention could be interpreted so as to accord with anything we may choose to do. So there can be neither accord, nor conflict. This is what Wittgenstein said in §201.

Wittgenstein's sceptical problem is related to some work of two other recent writers who show little direct influence from Wittgenstein. Both have already been mentioned above. The first is W. V. Quine,[37] whose well-known theses of the indeterminacy of translation and the inscrutability of reference also question whether there are any objective facts as to what we mean. If I may anticipate matters that the present exposition has not yet introduced, Quine's emphasis on agreement is obviously congenial to Wittgenstein's view.[38] So

---

[37] See pp. 14–15 above, and note 10.

[38] For 'agreement' and the related notion of 'form of life' in Wittgenstein, see pp. 96–8 below. In *Word and Object*, p. 27, Quine characterizes language as "the complex of present dispositions to verbal behavior, in which speakers of the same language have perforce come to resemble one another"; also see *Word and Object*, §2, pp. 5–8. Some of the major

is his rejection of any notion that inner 'ideas' or 'meanings' guide our linguistic behavior. However, there are differences. As I have remarked above, Quine bases his argument from the outset on behavioristic premises. He would never emphasize introspective thought experiments in the way Wittgenstein does, and he does not think of views that posit a private inner world as in need of elaborate refutation. For Quine, the untenability of any such views should be obvious to anyone who accepts a modern scientific outlook. Further, since Quine sees the philosophy of language within a hypothetical framework of behavioristic psychology, he thinks of problems about meaning as problems of disposition to behavior. This orientation seems to have consequences for the form of Quine's problem as opposed to Wittgenstein's. The important problem for Wittgenstein is that my present mental state does not appear to determine what I *ought* to do in the future. Although I may *feel* (now) that something in my head corresponding to the word 'plus' mandates a determinate response to any new pair of arguments, in fact nothing in my head does so. Alluding to one of Wittgenstein's earliest examples, 'ostensive' learning of the color word 'sepia' (§§28–30),[39] Quine protests against Wittgenstein that, given our 'inborn propensity to find one stimulation qualitatively more akin to a second stimulation than to a third' and sufficient conditioning 'to eliminate wrong generalizations', eventually the term will be learnt: ". . . in principle nothing more is needed in learning 'sepia' than in any conditioning or induction."[40] By "learning 'sepia'", Quine means developing the right disposition to apply 'sepia' in particular cases. It should be clear from Wittgenstein's text that he too is aware, indeed emphasizes, that in practice there need be no difficulty

concepts of *Word and Object*, such as that of 'observation sentence', depend on this uniformity in the community. Nevertheless, agreement seems to have a more crucial role in Wittgenstein's philosophy than in Quine's.

[39] This example is discussed below. See pp. 83–4 and note 72.

[40] Quine, *Ontological Relativity and Other Essays*, p. 31.

in this sense about the learning of 'sepia'. The fundamental problem, as I have stated it earlier, is different: whether my actual dispositions are 'right' or not, is there anything that mandates what they *ought* to be? Since Quine formulates the issues dispositionally, this problem cannot be stated within his framework. For Quine, since any fact as to whether I mean plus or quus will show up in my behavior, there is no question, given my disposition, as to what I mean.

It has already been argued above that such a formulation of the issues seems inadequate. My actual dispositions are not infallible, nor do they cover all of the infinitely many cases of the addition table. However, since Quine does see the issues in terms of dispositions, he is concerned to show that even if dispositions were ideally seen as infallible and covering all cases, there are still questions of interpretation that are left undetermined. First, he argues (roughly) that the interpretation of sufficiently 'theoretical' utterances, not direct observation reports, is undetermined even by all my ideal dispositions. Further, he seeks to show by examples such as 'rabbit' and 'rabbit-stage' that, even given fixed interpretation of our sentences as wholes and certainly given all our ideal dispositions to behavior, the interpretation (reference) of various lexical items is still not fixed.[41] These are interesting claims, distinct from Wittgenstein's. For those of us who are not as behavioristically inclined as Quine, Wittgenstein's problem may lead to a new look at Quine's theses. Given Quine's own formulation of his theses, it appears open to a non-behaviorist to regard his arguments, *if* he accepts them, as demonstrations that any behavioristic account of meaning must be inadequate – it cannot even distinguish between a word meaning rabbit and one meaning rabbit-stage. But if Wittgenstein is right, and no amount of access to my mind can reveal whether I mean plus or quus, may the same not hold for rabbit and rabbit-stage? So perhaps Quine's problem arises even for non-behaviorists. This is not the place to explore the matter.

[41] Roughly, the first assertion is the 'indeterminacy of translation', while the second is the 'inscrutability of reference'.

Nelson Goodman's discussion of the 'new riddle of induction' also deserves comparison with Wittgenstein's work.[42] Indeed, although Quine, like Wittgenstein, and unlike Goodman in his treatment of the 'new riddle', directly concerns himself with a sceptical doubt about meaning, the basic strategy of Goodman's treatment of the 'new riddle' is strikingly close to Wittgenstein's sceptical arguments. In this respect, his discussion is much closer to Wittgenstein's scepticism than is Quine's treatment of 'indeterminacy'. Although our paradigm of Wittgenstein's problem was formulated for a mathematical problem, it was emphasized that it is completely general and can be applied to any rule or word. In particular, if it were formulated for the language of color impressions, as Wittgenstein himself suggests, Goodman's 'grue', or something similar, would play the role of 'quus'.[43] But the problem would not be Goodman's about induction – "Why not predict that grass, which has been grue in the past, will be grue in the future?" – but Wittgenstein's about meaning: "Who is to say that in the past I didn't mean grue by 'green', so that now I should call the sky, not the grass, 'green'?" Although Goodman concentrates on the problem about induction and largely ignores the problem about meaning,[44] his discussions are occasionally suggestive for

[42] See the reference cited in n. 14. See also the papers in part VII ("Induction") in *Problems and Projects* (Bobbs-Merrill, Indianapolis and New York, 1972, xii + 463 pp.)

[43] For 'grue', see page 20 and footnotes 14 and 15 above. My memory about my own thought processes years ago is weak, but it seems likely that I may have been inspired to formulate Wittgenstein's problem in terms of 'quus' by Goodman's analogous use of 'grue'. I do remember that, at the time I first thought about the problem, I was struck by the analogy between Wittgenstein's discussion and Goodman's (as others have been as well).

[44] In part Goodman's discussion of the problem seems to presuppose that the extension of each predicate ('green', 'grue'), etc., is known, and that this question does not itself get entangled in the 'new riddle of induction'. Sydney Shoemaker, "On Projecting the Unprojectible," *The Philosophical Review*, vol. 84 (1975), pp. 178–219, questions whether such a separation is possible (see his concluding paragraph). I have not yet made a careful study of Shoemaker's argument.

Wittgenstein's problem as well.[45] In fact, I personally suspect that serious consideration of Goodman's problem, as he formulates it, may prove impossible without consideration of Wittgenstein's.[46]

[45] See his "Positionality and Pictures," *The Philosophical Review*, vol. 69 (1960), pp. 523–5, reprinted in *Problems and Projects*, pp. 402–4. See also Ullian, "More on 'Grue' and Grue," and *Problems and Projects*, pp. 408–9 (comments on Judith Thompson).

"Seven Strictures on Similarity," *Problems and Projects*, pp. 437–46, has in places a Wittgensteinian flavor. For Goodman, as for Wittgenstein, what we call 'similar' (for Wittgenstein: even 'the same') is exhibited in our own practice and cannot explain it. (Wittgenstein's view is expounded below.)

One issue arises here. Does Wittgenstein's position depend on a denial of 'absolute similarity'? To the extent that we use 'similarity' simply to *endorse* the way we actually go on, it does. But it is important to see that, even if 'absolutely similar' had a fixed meaning in English, and 'similar' did not need to be filled in by a specification of the 'respects' in which things are similar, the sceptical problem would not be solved. When I learn 'plus', I could not simply give myself some finite number of examples and continue: 'Act similarly when confronted with any addition problem in the future.' Suppose that, on the ordinary meaning of 'similar' this construction is completely determinate, and that one does not hold the doctrine that various alternative ways of acting can be called 'similar', depending on how 'similar' is filled out by speaking of a respect in which one or another way of acting can be called 'similar' to what I did before. Even so, the sceptic can argue that by 'similar' I meant *quimilar*, where two actions are quimilar if . . . See also the discussion of 'relative identity', note 13 above.

[46] Briefly: Goodman insists that there is no sense that does not beg the question according to which 'grue' is 'temporal', or 'positional', and 'green' is not; if either of the pairs 'blue-green' and 'grue-bleen' is taken as primitive, the predicates of the other pair are 'temporally' definable in terms of it (see *Fact, Fiction, and Forecast*, pp. 77–80). Nevertheless, intuitively it does seem clear that 'grue' is positional in a sense that 'green' is not. Perhaps that sense can be brought out by the fact that 'green', but not 'grue', is learned (learnable?) ostensively by a sufficient number of samples, without reference to time. It would seem that a reply to this argument should take the form. "Who is to say that it is not 'grue' that others (or even, myself in the past?) learned by such ostensive training?" But this leads directly to Wittgenstein's problem. The papers cited in the previous footnote are relevant. (It is true, however, that problems like Goodman's can arise for competing predicates that do not appear, even intuitively, to be defined positionally.)

Wittgenstein has invented a new form of scepticism. Personally I am inclined to regard it as the most radical and original sceptical problem that philosophy has seen to date, one that only a highly unusual cast of mind could have produced. Of course he does not wish to leave us with his problem, but to solve it: the sceptical conclusion is insane and intolerable. It is his solution, I will argue, that contains the argument against 'private language'; for allegedly, the solution will not admit such a language. But it is important to see that his achievement in posing this problem stands on its own, independently of the value of his own solution of it and the resultant argument against private language. For, if we see Wittgenstein's problem as a real one, it is clear that he has often been read from the wrong perspective. Readers, my previous self certainly included, have often been inclined to wonder: "How can he prove private language impossible? How can I possibly have any difficulty identifying my own sensations? And if there were a difficulty, how could 'public' criteria help me? I must be in pretty bad shape if I needed external *help* to identify my own sensations!"[47] But if I am right, a proper

---

[47] Especially for those who know some of the literature on the 'private language argument', an elaboration of this point may be useful. Much of this literature, basing itself on Wittgenstein's discussions following §243, thinks that without some external check on my identification of my own sensations, I would have no way of knowing that I have identified a given sensation correctly (in accord with my previous intentions). (The question has been interpreted to be, "How do I know I am right that this is pain?", or it might be, "How do I know that I am applying the right rule, using 'pain' as I had intended it?" See note 21 above.) But, it is argued, if I have no way of knowing (on one of these interpretations) whether I am making the right identification, it is meaningless to speak of an identification at all. To the extent that I rely on my own impressions or memories of what I meant by various sensation signs for support, I have no way of quelling these doubts. Only others, who recognize the correctness of my identification through my external behavior, can provide an appropriate external check.

A great deal could be said about the argument just obscurely summarized, which is not easy to follow even on the basis of longer presentations in the literature. But here I wish to mention one reaction: If

(handwritten at top: ① I do not identify my visual impressions (wine-tasting?) arbitrarily ∴② I do not doubt my ability to identify impressions)

I really were in doubt as to whether I could identify any sensations correctly, how would a connection of my sensations with external behavior, or confirmation by others, be of any help? Surely I can identify that the relevant external behavior has taken place, or that others are confirming that I do indeed have the sensation in question, only because I can identify relevant <u>sensory impressions</u> (of the behavior, or of others confirming that I have identified the sensation correctly). My ability to *(handwritten: not W.)* make any identification of any external phenomenon rests on my ability to identify relevant sensory (especially visual) impressions. If I were to entertain a *general* <u>doubt</u> of my ability to identify any of my own mental states, it would be impossible to escape from it. *(handwritten: not the question ←)*

It is in this sense that it may appear that the argument against private language supposes that I need external *help* to identify my own sensations. For many presentations of the argument make it appear to depend on such a general doubt of the correctness of all my identifications of inner states. It is argued that since any identification I make needs some kind of verification for correctness, a verification of one identification of an inner state by another such identification simply raises the very same question (whether I am making a correct identification of my sensations) over again. As A. J. Ayer, in his well known exchange with Rush Rhees ("Can there be a Private Language?" *Proceedings of the Aristotelian Society*, Supp. Vol. 28 (1954), pp. 63–94, reprinted in Pitcher (ed.), *Wittgenstein: The Philosophical Investigations*, pp. 251–85, see especially p. 256), <u>summarizes</u> the argument, "His claim to recognize the object [the *(handwritten: Ayer's interp.)* sensation], his belief that it really is the same, is not to be accepted unless it can be backed by further evidence. Apparently, too, this evidence must be public . . . Merely to check one private sensation by another would not be enough. For if one cannot be trusted to recognize one of them, neither can one be trusted to recognize the other." The argument concludes that I can make a genuine verification of the correctness of my identification only if I break out of the circle of 'private checks' to some publicly accessible evidence. But if I were so sceptical as to doubt *all* my identifications of inner states , how could anything public be of any help? *(handwritten: It does not)* Does not my recognition of anything public depend on the recognition of *(handwritten: No)* <u>my inner states</u>? As Ayer puts it (immediately following the earlier quotation), "But unless there is some thing that one is allowed to recognize, no test can ever be completed . . . I check my memory of the time at which the train is due to leave by visualizing a page of the time-table; and I am required to check this in its turn by looking up the page. [He is alluding to §265.] But unless I can trust my eyesight at this point, unless I can recognize the figures that I see written down, I am still no better off . . . Let the object to which I am attempting to refer be as public as you please . . . my assurance that I am using the word correctly . . . must in the end rest on the <u>testimony</u> of the senses. It is through

(handwritten left margin: Presupposes Lockean view of lang. that W. is rejecting)

(handwritten bottom: ≠ identifying some inner state)

orientation would be the opposite. The main problem is *not*, "How can we show private language – or some other special form of language – to be *impossible?*"; rather it is, "How can we show *any language* at all (public, private, or what-have-you) to be *possible?*"[48] It is not that calling a sensation 'pain' is easy, and Wittgenstein must invent a difficulty.[49] On the contrary, Wittgenstein's main problem is that it appears that he has shown *all* language, *all* concept formation, to be impossible, indeed unintelligible.

It is important and illuminating to compare Wittgenstein's new form of scepticism with the classical scepticism of Hume; there are important analogies between the two. Both develop a sceptical paradox, based on questioning a certain *nexus* from past to future. Wittgenstein questions the nexus between past 'intention' or 'meanings' and present practice: for example, between my past 'intentions' with regard to 'plus' and my present computation '$68+57=125$'. Hume questions two other nexuses, related to each other: the causal nexus whereby a past event necessitates a future one, and the inductive inferential nexus from the past to the future.

---

hearing what other people say, or through seeing what they write, or observing their movements, that I am enabled to conclude that their use of the word agrees with mine. But if without further ado I can recognize such noises or shapes or movements, why can I not also recognize a private sensation?"

Granted that the private language argument is presented simply in this form, the objection seems cogent. Certainly it once seemed to me on some basis such as this that the argument against private language *could* not be right. Traditional views, which are very plausible unless they are decisively rebutted, hold that all identifications rest on the identification of sensations. The sceptical interpretation of the argument in this essay, which does not allow the notion of an identification to be taken for granted, makes the issue very different. See the discussion, on pp. 67–8 below, of an analogous objection to Hume's analysis of causation.

[48] So put, the problem has an obvious Kantian flavor.

[49] See especially the discussions of 'green' and 'grue' above, which plainly could carry over to pain (let 'pickle' apply to pains before *t*, and tickles thereafter!); but it is clear enough by now that the problem is completely general.

The analogy is obvious. It has been obscured for several reasons. First, the Humean and the Wittgensteinian problems are of course distinct and independent, though analogous. Second, Wittgenstein shows little interest in or sympathy with Hume: he has been quoted as saying that he could not read Hume because he found it "a torture".[50] Furthermore, Hume is the prime source of some ideas on the nature of mental states that Wittgenstein is most concerned to attack.[51] Finally (and probably most important), Wittgenstein never avows, and almost surely would not avow, the label 'sceptic', as Hume explicitly did. Indeed, he has often appeared to be a 'common-sense' philosopher, anxious to defend our ordinary conceptions and dissolve traditional philosophical doubts. Is it not Wittgenstein who held that philosophy only states what everyone admits?

Yet even here the difference between Wittgenstein and Hume should not be exaggerated. Even Hume has an important strain, dominant in some of his moods, that the philosopher never questions ordinary beliefs. Asked whether he "be really one of those sceptics, who hold that all is uncertain", Hume replies "that this question is entirely superfluous, and that neither I, nor any other person, was ever sincerely and constantly of that opinion".[52] Even more forcefully, discussing the problem of the external world: "We

[50] Karl Britton, "Portrait of a Philosopher," *The Listener*, LIII, no. 1372 (June 16, 1955), p. 1072, quoted by George Pitcher, *The Philosophy of Wittgenstein* (Prentice Hall, Englewood Cliffs, NJ, 1964, viii+340 pp), p. 325.

[51] Much of Wittgenstein's argument can be regarded as an attack on characteristically Humean (or classical empiricist) ideas. Hume posits an introspectible qualitative state for each of our psychological states (an 'impression'). Further, he thinks that an appropriate 'impression' or 'image' can constitute an 'idea', without realizing that an image in no way tells us how it is to be applied. (See the discussion of determining the meaning of 'green' with an image on p. 20 above and the corresponding discussion of the cube on pp. 42–3 above.) Of course the Wittgensteinian paradox is, among other things, a strong protest against such suppositions.

[52] David Hume, *A Treatise of Human Nature* (ed. L. A. Selby-Bigge,

may well ask, *What causes induce us to believe in the existence of body?* but 'tis in vain to ask, *Whether there be body or not?* That is a point, which we must take for granted in all our reasonings."[53] Yet this oath of fealty to common sense begins a section that otherwise looks like an argument that the common conception of material objects is irreparably incoherent!

When Hume is in a mood to respect his professed determination never to deny or doubt our common beliefs, in what does his 'scepticism' consist? First, in a sceptical *account* of the causes of these beliefs; and second, in sceptical analyses of our common notions. In some ways Berkeley, who did not regard his own views as sceptical, may offer an even better analogy to Wittgenstein. At first blush, Berkeley, with his denial of matter, and of any objects 'outside the mind' seems to be *denying* our common beliefs; and for many of us the impression persists through later blushes. But not for Berkeley. For him, the impression that the common man is committed to matter and to objects outside the mind derives from an erroneous metaphysical interpretation of common talk. When the common man speaks of an 'external material object' he does not really mean (as we might say *sotto voce*) an *external material object* but rather he means something like 'an idea produced in me independently of my will'.[54]

Clarendon Press, Oxford, 1888), Book I, Part IV, Section I (p. 183 in the Selby-Bigge edition).

[53] Hume, *ibid.*, Book I, Part IV, Section II (p. 187 in the Selby-Bigge edition). Hume's occasional affinities to 'ordinary language' philosophy should not be overlooked. Consider the following: "Those philosophers, who have divided human reason into *knowledge and probability*, and have defined the first to be *that evidence, which arises from the comparison of ideas*, are obliged to comprehend all our arguments from causes or effects under the general term of probability. But tho' everyone be free to use his terms in what sense he pleases . . . 'tis however certain, that in common discourse we readily affirm, that many arguments from causation exceed probability, and may be received as a superior kind of evidence. One would appear ridiculous, who would say, that 'tis only probable the sun will rise tomorrow, or that all men must dye . . ." (*ibid.*, Book I, Part III, Section XI, p. 124 in the Selby-Bigge edition).

[54] George Berkeley, *The Principles of Human Knowledge*, §§29–34. Of course

Berkeley's stance is not uncommon in philosophy. The philosopher advocates a view apparently in patent contradiction to common sense. Rather than repudiating common sense, he asserts that the conflict comes from a philosophical misinterpretation of common language – sometimes he adds that the misinterpretation is encouraged by the 'superficial form' of ordinary speech. He offers his own analysis of the relevant common assertions, one that shows that they do not really say what they seem to say. For Berkeley this philosophical strategy is central to his work. To the extent that Hume claims that he merely analyses common sense and does not oppose it, he invokes the same strategy as well. The practice can hardly be said to have ceased today.[55]

Personally I think such philosophical claims are almost invariably suspect. What the claimant calls a 'misleading philosophical misconstrual' of the ordinary statement is probably the natural and correct understanding. The real misconstrual comes when the claimant continues, "All the ordinary man really means is . . ." and gives a sophisticated analysis compatible with his own philosophy. Be this as it may, the important point for present purposes is that Wittgenstein makes a Berkeleyan claim of this kind. For – as we shall see – his solution to his own sceptical problem begins by agreeing with the sceptics that there is no 'superlative fact' (§192) about my mind that constitutes my meaning addition by 'plus' and determines in advance what I should do to accord with this meaning. But, he claims (in §§183–93), the appearance that our ordinary concept of meaning demands such a fact is based on a philosophical misconstrual – albeit a natural one –

---

the characterization may be oversimplified, but it suffices for present purposes.

[55] It is almost 'analytic' that I cannot produce a common contemporary example that would not meet with vigorous opposition. Those who hold the cited view would argue that, in this case, their analyses of ordinary usage are really correct. I have no desire to enter into an irrelevant controversy here, but I myself find that many of the 'topic–neutral' analyses of discourse about the mind proposed by contemporary materialists are just the other side of the Berkeleyan coin.

of such ordinary expressions as 'he meant such-and-such', 'the steps are determined by the formula', and the like. How Wittgenstein construes these expressions we shall see presently. For the moment let us only remark that Wittgenstein thinks that any construal that looks for something in my present mental state to differentiate between my meaning addition or quaddition, or that will consequently show that in the future I should say '125' when asked about '68+57', *is a* misconstrual and attributes to the ordinary man a notion of meaning that *is* refuted by the sceptical argument. "We are," he says in §194 – note that Berkeley could have said just the same thing! – "like savages, primitive people, who hear the expressions of civilized men, put a false interpretation on them, and then draw the queerest conclusions from it." Maybe so. Personally I can only report that, in spite of Wittgenstein's assurances, the 'primitive' interpretation often sounds rather good to me . . .

In his *Enquiry*, after he has developed his "Sceptical Doubts Concerning the Operations of the Understanding", Hume gives his "Sceptical Solution of These Doubts". What is a 'sceptical' solution? Call a proposed solution to a sceptical philosophical problem a *straight* solution if it shows that on closer examination the scepticism proves to be unwarranted; an elusive or complex argument proves the thesis the sceptic doubted. Descartes gave a 'straight' solution in this sense to his own philosophical doubts. An *a priori* justification of inductive reasoning, and an analysis of the causal relation as a genuine necessary connection or nexus between pairs of events, would be straight solutions of Hume's problems of induction and causation, respectively. A *sceptical* solution of a sceptical philosophical problem begins on the contrary by conceding that the sceptic's negative assertions are unanswerable. Nevertheless our ordinary practice or belief is justified because – contrary appearances notwithstanding – it need not require the justification the sceptic has shown to be untenable. And much of the value of the sceptical argument consists precisely in the fact that he has shown that an ordinary practice, if it is to be defended at all, cannot be defended in a certain way. A sceptical solution may also involve – in the manner suggested above – a sceptical analysis or account of ordinary beliefs to rebut their *prima facie* reference to a metaphysical absurdity.

The rough outlines of Hume's sceptical solution to his problem are well known.[56] Not an *a priori* argument, but custom, is the source of our inductive inferences. If *A* and *B* are two types of events which we have seen constantly conjoined, then we are conditioned – Hume is a grandfather of this modern psychological notion – to expect an event of type *B* on being presented with one of type *A*. To say of a particular event *a* that it caused another event *b* is to place these two events under two types, *A* and *B*, which we expect to be constantly conjoined in the future as they were in the past. The idea of necessary connection comes from the 'feeling of customary transition' between our ideas of these event types.

The philosophical merits of the Humean solution are not our present concern. Our purpose is to use the analogy with the Humean solution to illuminate Wittgenstein's solution to his own problem. For comparative purposes one further consequence of Hume's sceptical solution should be noted. Naively, one might suppose that whether a particular event *a* causes another particular event *b*, is an issue solely involving the events *a* and *b* alone (and their relations), and involves no other events. If Hume is right, this is not so. Even if God were to look at the events, he would discern nothing relating them other than that one succeeds the other. Only when the particular events *a* and *b* are thought of as subsumed under two respective event types, *A* and *B*, which are related by a generalization that *all* events of type *A* are followed by events of type *B*, can *a* be said to 'cause' *b*. When the events *a* and *b* are

---

[56] Writing this sentence, I find myself prey to an appropriate fear that (some) experts in Hume and Berkeley will not approve of some particular thing that I say about these philosophers here. I have made no careful study of them for the purpose of this paper. Rather a crude and fairly conventional account of the 'rough outlines' of their views is used for purposes of comparison with Wittgenstein.

considered by themselves alone, no causal notions are applicable. This Humean conclusion might be called: the impossibility of private causation.

Can one reasonably protest: surely there is nothing the event *a* can do with the *help* of other events of the same type that it cannot do by itself! Indeed, to say that *a*, by itself, is a sufficient cause of *b* is to say that, had the rest of the universe been removed, *a* still would have produced *b*! Intuitively this may well be so, but the intuitive objection ignores Hume's sceptical argument. The whole point of the sceptical argument is that the common notion of one event 'producing' another, on which the objection relies, is in jeopardy. It appears that there is no such relation as 'production' at all, that the causal relation is fictive. After the sceptical argument has been seen to be unanswerable on its own terms, a sceptical solution is offered, containing all we can salvage of the notion of causation. It just is a feature of this analysis that causation makes no sense when applied to two isolated events, with the rest of the universe removed. Only inasmuch as these events are thought of as instances of event types related by a regularity can they be thought of as causally connected. If two particular events were somehow so *sui generis* that it was logically excluded that they be placed under any (plausibly natural) event types, causal notions would not be applicable to them.

Of course I am suggesting that Wittgenstein's argument against private language has a structure similar to Hume's argument against private causation. Wittgenstein also states a sceptical paradox. Like Hume, he accepts his own sceptical argument and offers a 'sceptical solution' to overcome the appearance of paradox. His solution involves a sceptical interpretation of what is involved in such ordinary assertions as "Jones means addition by '+'." The impossibility of private language emerges as a corollary of his sceptical solution of his own paradox, as does the impossibility of 'private causation' in Hume. It turns out that the sceptical solution does not allow us to speak of a single individual, considered by himself and in isolation, as ever meaning anything. Once again an objection based on an intuitive feeling that no one else can affect what I mean by a given symbol ignores the sceptical argument that undermines any such naive intuition about meaning.

I have said that Wittgenstein's solution to his problem is a sceptical one. He does not give a 'straight' solution, pointing out to the silly sceptic a hidden fact he overlooked, a condition in the world which constitutes my meaning addition by 'plus'. In fact, he agrees with his own hypothetical sceptic that there is no such fact, no such condition in either the 'internal' or the 'external' world. Admittedly, I am expressing Wittgenstein's view more straightforwardly than he would ordinarily allow himself to do. For in denying that there is any such fact, might we not be expressing a philosophical thesis that doubts or denies something everyone admits? We do not wish to doubt or deny that when people speak of themselves and others as meaning something by their words, as following rules, they do so with perfect right. We do not even wish to deny the propriety of an ordinary use of the phrase 'the fact that Jones meant addition by such-and-such a symbol', and indeed such expressions do have perfectly ordinary uses. We merely wish to deny the existence of the 'superlative fact' that philosophers misleadingly attach to such ordinary forms of words, not the propriety of the forms of words themselves.

It is for this reason that I conjectured above (p. 5), that Wittgenstein's professed inability to write a work with conventionally organized arguments and conclusions stems at least in part, not from personal and stylistic proclivities, but from the nature of his work. Had Wittgenstein – contrary to his notorious and cryptic maxim in §128 – stated the outcomes of his conclusions in the form of definite theses, it would have been very difficuilt to avoid formulating his doctrines in a form that consists in apparent sceptical denials of our ordinary assertions. Berkeley runs into similar difficulties. Partly he avoids them by stating his thesis as the denial of the existence of 'matter', and claiming that 'matter' is a bit of philosophical jargon, not expressive of our common sense view. Nevertheless he is forced at one point to say – apparently contrary to his usual official doctrine – that he denies a doctrine 'strangely prevailing amongst men'.[57] If, on the other hand, we do not state our conclusions in the form of broad philosophical theses, it is easier to avoid the danger of a denial of any ordinary belief, even if our imaginary interlocutor (e.g. §189; see also §195)[58] accuses us of doing so. Whenever our opponent insists on the perfect propriety of an ordinary form of expression (e.g. that 'the steps are determined by the formula', 'the future application is already present'), we can insist that if these expressions are properly understood, we agree. The danger comes when we try to give a precise formulation of exactly what it is that we *are* denying – *what* 'erroneous interpretation' our opponent is placing on ordinary means of expression. It may be hard to do this without producing yet another statement that, we must admit, is *still* 'perfectly all right, properly understood'.[59]

So Wittgenstein, perhaps cagily, might well disapprove of the straightforward formulation given here. Nevertheless I choose to be so bold as to say: Wittgenstein holds, with the

[57] Berkeley, *The Principles of Human Knowledge*, §4. Of course Berkeley might mean that the prevalence of the doctrine stems from the influence of philosophical theory rather than common sense, as indeed he asserts in the next section.

[58] §189: "But *are* the steps then *not* determined by the algebraic formula?" In spite of Wittgenstein's interpretation within his own philosophy of the ordinary phrase "the steps are determined by the formula", the impression persists that the interlocutor's characterization of his view is really correct. See §195: "But I don't mean that what I do now (in grasping a sense) determines the future use *causally* and as a matter of experience, but that in a *queer* way, the use itself is in some sense present," which are the words of the interlocutor, and the bland reply, "But of course it is, 'in *some* sense'! Really the only thing wrong with what you say is the expression "in a queer way". The rest is all right; and the sentence only seems queer when one imagines a different language-game for it from the one in which we actually use it."

[59] An example of the kind of tension that can be involved appeared already above – see pp. 49–51 and note 33.

sceptic, that there is no fact as to whether I mean plus or quus. But if this is to be conceded to the sceptic, is this not the end of the matter? What *can* be said on behalf of our ordinary attributions of meaningful language to ourselves and to others? Has not the incredible and self-defeating conclusion, that all language is meaningless, already been drawn?

In reply we must say something about the change in Wittgenstein's philosophy of language from the *Tractatus* to the *Investigations*. Although in detail the *Tractatus* is among the most difficult of philosophical works, its rough outlines are well known. To each sentence there corresponds a (possible) fact. If such a fact, obtains, the sentence is true; if not, false. For atomic sentences, the relation between a sentence and the fact it alleges is one of a simple correspondence or isomorphism. The sentence contains names, corresponding to objects. An atomic sentence is itself a fact, putting the names in a certain relation; and it says that (there is a corresponding fact that) the corresponding objects are in the same relation. Other sentences are (finite or infinite) truth-functions of these. Even though the details of this theory have struck some as an implausible attempt to give natural language a chimerical *a priori* structure based on logical analysis alone, similar ideas, often advanced without any specific influence from the *Tractatus*, are much alive today.[60]

[60] Donald Davidson's influential and important theory of natural language has many features in common with the *Tractatus*, even if the underlying philosophy is different. Davidson argues that some simple, almost *a priori* considerations (not requiring detailed empirical investigation of specific natural languages) put strong constraints on the form of a theory of meaning for natural languages (it must be a finitely axiomatized Tarski-style theory of truth conditions). (Although the *form* of a theory is determined without detailed empirical investigation, for a particular language the specific theory adopted is supposed to require detailed empirical support.) The fact that a theory of meaning must have this form, it is argued, puts strong constraints on the logical form, or deep structure, of natural language – very probably that it ought to be close to classical extensional first order logic. All these ideas are close to the spirit of the *Tractatus*. In particular, like the *Tractatus*, Davidson holds (i) that truth conditions are a key element in a theory of language; (ii) that the

The simplest, most basic idea of the *Tractatus* can hardly be dismissed: a declarative sentence gets its meaning by virtue of its *truth conditions*, by virtue of its correspondence to facts that must obtain if it is true. For example, "the cat is on the mat" is understood by those speakers who realize that it is true if and only if a certain cat is on a certain mat; it is false otherwise. The presence of the cat on the mat is a fact or condition-in-the-world that would make the sentence true (express a truth) if it obtained.

So stated, the *Tractatus* picture of the meaning of declarative

---

uncovering of a hidden deep structure of language is crucial to a proper theory of interpretation; (iii) that the form of the deep structure is constrained in advance by theoretical, quasi-logical considerations; (iv) that, in particular, the constraints show that the deep structure has a logical form close to that of a formal language of symbolic logic; (v) that, in particular, sentences are built up from 'atoms' by logical operators; (vi) that, in particular, the deep structure of natural language is extensional in spite of the misleading appearances of surface structure. All these ideas of the *Tractatus* are repudiated in the *Investigations*, which is hostile to any attempt to analyze language by uncovering a hidden deep structure. In this last respect, modern transformational linguistics, since Noam Chomsky, has been closer to the *Tractatus* than to the *Investigations*. (But for transformational grammarians, even the form of the theory is established by specific empirical considerations requiring detailed investigation of specific natural languages.)

See also the programs of the linguists who called themselves 'generative semanticists' and of Richard Montague. Of course many of the ideas of the *Tractatus*, or of 'logical atomism', have not been revived in any of these theories.

(Note: In recent transformational linguistics, 'deep structure' has a specific technical meaning. 'Generative semanticists' made the repudiation of 'deep structure' a key plank of their platform. In the preceding, it is best to take 'deep structure' in the general sense of 'underlying' structure. Anyone whose theory of language leads him to applaud the doctrine of *Tractatus* 4.002 – that the understanding of language involves countless tacit conventions, invisible to the naked eye, that disguise form – believes in deep structure in this broad sense. 'Deep structure' in the specific sense was a special theory of deep structure thus broadly defined; that is one reason why it was an appropriate term. Most recent linguistic theories that rejected 'deep structure' in the specific sense accepted it in the broader sense.)

sentences may seem not only natural but even tautological. Nonetheless, as Dummett says, "the *Investigations* contains implicitly a rejection of the classical (realist) Frege–*Tractatus* view that the general form of explanation of meaning is a statement of the truth conditions".[61] In the place of this view, Wittgenstein proposes an alternative rough general picture. (To call it an alternative *theory* probably goes too far. Wittgenstein disclaims (§65) any intent of offering a general account of language to rival that of the *Tractatus*. Rather we have different activities related to each other in various ways.) Wittgenstein replaces the question, "What must be the case for this sentence to be true?" by two others: first, "Under what conditions may this form of words be appropriately asserted (or denied)?"; second, given an answer to the first question, "What is the role, and the utility, in our lives of our practice of asserting (or denying) the form of words under these conditions?"

Of course Wittgenstein does not confine himself to declarative sentences, and hence to assertion and denial, as I have just done. On the contrary, any reader of the earlier parts of *Philosophical Investigations* will be aware that he is strongly concerned to deny any special primacy to assertion, or to sentences in the indicative mood. (See his early examples "Slab!", "Pillar!", etc.) This in itself plays an important role in his repudiation of the classical realist picture. Since the indicative mood is not taken as in any sense primary or basic, it becomes more plausible that the linguistic role even of utterances in the indicative mood that superficially look like assertions need not be one of 'stating facts'.[62] Thus, if we speak properly, we should not speak of conditions of 'asser-

[61] Dummett, "Wittgenstein's Philosophy of Mathematics," p. 348 in the original; reprinted in Pitcher (ed.), *Wittgenstein: The Philosophical Investigations*, pp. 446–7.

[62] See, for example, §304, where Wittgenstein is dealing with sensation language: "The paradox disappears only if we make a radical break with the idea that language . . . always serves the same purpose: to convey thoughts – which may be about houses, pains, good and evil, or anything else you please."

tion', but rather, more generally, of the conditions when a move (a form of linguistic expression) is to be made in the 'language game'. If, however, we allow ourselves to adopt an oversimplified terminology more appropriate to a special range of cases, we can say that Wittgenstein proposes a picture of language based, not on *truth conditions*, but on *assertability conditions* or *justification conditions*:[63] under what circumstances are we allowed to make a given assertion? Pictures, indeed explicit theories, of this kind are hardly unknown before

---

[63] Speaking of 'justification conditions' does not suggest the primacy of the indicative mood as much as 'assertability conditions', but it has its own drawbacks. For Wittgenstein, there is an important class of cases where a use of language properly has no independent justification other than the speaker's inclination to speak thus on that occasion (e.g. saying that one is in pain). In such cases, Wittgenstein says (§289), "To use a word without a justification (*Rechtfertigung*) does not mean to use it *zu Unrecht.*" Anscombe's translation of '*zu Unrecht*' is not consistent. In her translation of *Philosophical Investigations*, §289, she translates it 'without right'. However, in her translation of *Remarks on the Foundations of Mathematics*, V, §33 [VII, §40], where almost exactly the same German sentence occurs, she translates it as 'wrongfully'. The German–English dictionary I have at hand (Wildhagen-Heraucourt, Brandstetter Verlag, Wiesbaden, and Allen and Unwin, London, 6th ed., 1962), translates '*zu Unrecht*' as 'unjustly, unfairly'; '*Unrecht*' in general is an 'injustice' or a 'wrong'. All this is reasonably consistent with 'wrongfully' but gives little support to 'without right', even though the idea that we have a 'right' to use a word in certain circumstances without 'justification' ('*Rechtfertigung*') is obviously in harmony with the point Wittgenstein is trying to make. However, by '*zu Unrecht*' Wittgenstein seems to mean that the use of a word without independent justification need not be a 'wrongful' use of the word – one without proper epistemic or linguistic support. On the contrary, it is essential to the workings of our language that, in some cases, such a use of language is perfectly proper. When we use the terminology of 'justification conditions', we must construe them to include such cases (where Wittgenstein would say there is no 'justification'). (Simply 'wrongly', might be a more idiomatic translation than 'wrongfully'. 'Without right' sounds to me too much as if a difficult new technical term is being introduced. The point is that '*zu Unrecht*', being a fairly ordinary German expression, should not be rendered so as to appear to be an unusual technical expression in English.) See also pp. 87–8 and note 75 below.

Wittgenstein and probably influenced him. The positivist verification theory of meaning is one of this kind. So, in a more special context, is the intuitionistic account of mathematical statements. (The classical mathematician's emphasis on truth conditions is replaced by an emphasis on provability conditions.) But of course Wittgenstein's rough picture should not be identified with either of these. Its second component is distinct: granted that our language game permits a certain 'move' (assertion) under certain specifiable conditions, what is the role in our lives of such permission? Such a role must exist if this aspect of the language game is not to be idle.

Wittgenstein's alternative picture of language is already clearly suggested in the very first section of *Philosophical Investigations*. Many philosophers of mathematics – in agreement with the Augustinian conception of 'object and name' – ask such questions as, "What entities ('numbers') are denoted by numerals? What relations among these entities ('facts') correspond to numerical statements?" (Nominalistically inclined philosophers would counter, sceptically, "Can we really believe that there are such entities?") As against such a 'Platonist' conception of the problem, Wittgenstein asks that we discard any *a priori* conceptions and *look* ("Don't think, look!") at the circumstances under which numerical assertions are actually uttered, and at what roles such assertions play in our lives.[64] Suppose I go to the grocer with a slip marked 'five

---

[64] In some ways Frege can be taken to be the target here. It is he who insists on regarding numbers as *objects*, and on asking about the nature of these objects (even insisting that we can ask whether Julius Caesar is a number or not). On the other hand, the famous contextual principle of *Grundlagen der Arithmetik* (that one should ask for the signification of a sign only in the context of a sentence) and his emphasis in particular on asking how numerical expressions are actually applied are in the spirit of Wittgenstein's discussion. Perhaps the best conception of Wittgenstein's relation to Frege here is to say that Wittgenstein would regard the spirit of Frege's contextual principle as sound but would criticize Frege for using 'name of an object' as a catch-all for uses of language that are 'absolutely unlike' (§10).

red apples', and he hands over apples, reciting by heart the numerals up to five and handing over an apple as each numeral is intoned. It is under circumstances such as these that we are licensed to make utterances using numerals; the role and utility of such a license is obvious. In §§8–10, Wittgenstein imagines the letters of the alphabet, recited in alphabetical order, used in a miniature language game, just as the numbers are in this example. We have little inclination to wonder about the nature of the entities 'denoted' by the letters of the alphabet. Nevertheless, if they are used in the way described, they can properly be said to 'stand for numbers'. Indeed, to say words stand for (natural) numbers *is* to say that they are used as numerals, that is, used in the way described. Nevertheless the legitimacy, in its own way, of the expression 'stand for numbers' should not lead us to think of numerals as similar to expressions such as 'slab', 'pillar', and the like, except that the entities 'denoted' are not spatio-temporal. If the use of the expression 'stands for numbers' misleads in this way, it would be best to think in terms of another terminology, say, that an expression 'plays the role of a numeral'. This role, as Wittgenstein describes it, is plainly in strong *contrast* with the role of such expressions as 'slab', 'pillar', 'block', in the language games he describes in his early sections. (See §10.)

The case is a fine example of various aspects of Wittgenstein's technique in the *Investigations*. An important view in the philosophy of mathematics is suggested briefly almost *en passant*, almost hidden in a general discussion of the nature of language and 'language games'.[65] In the style discussed above,

[65] Paul Benacerraf, in "What Numbers Could Not Be," *The Philosophical Review*, vol. 74 (1963), pp. 47–73, see especially pp. 71–2, concludes with suggestions strikingly similar to Wittgenstein's though much of the preceding argumentation has no direct parallel in Wittgenstein. It is possible that one reason the resemblance of the views to those of a fairly well-known portion of the *Investigations* was not noticed is the *en passant* way Wittgenstein introduces the issue in the philosophy of mathematics in the context of a more general discussion. (Although I do not take it upon myself to criticize Wittgenstein in this essay, it seems to me that a great deal of further work must be done if one wishes to defend

Wittgenstein suggests that such an expression as 'stands for a number' is in order, but is dangerous if it is taken to make a certain metaphysical suggestion. In the sense this is intended by 'Platonists', one suspects him of *denying* that numerals stand for entities called 'numbers'. Most important for the present purpose, the case exemplifies the central questions he wishes to ask about the use of language. Do not look for 'entities' and 'facts' corresponding to numerical assertions, but look at the circumstances under which utterances involving numerals are made, and the utility of making them under these circumstances.

Now the replacement of truth conditions by justification conditions has a dual role in the *Investigations*. First, it offers a new approach to the problems of how language has meaning, contrasted with that of the *Tractatus*. But second, it can be applied to give an account of assertions about meaning themselves, regarded as assertions *within* our language. Recall Wittgenstein's sceptical conclusion: no facts, no truth conditions, correspond to statements such as "Jones means addition by '+'." (The present remarks about meaning and use do not in themselves provide such truth conditions. According to them, Jones now means addition by '+' if he presently intends to use the '+' sign in one way, quaddition if he intends to use it another way. But nothing is said to illuminate the question as to the nature of such an intention.)

Now if we suppose that facts, or truth conditions, are of the essence of meaningful assertion, it will follow from the sceptical conclusion that assertions that anyone ever means anything are meaningless. On the other hand, if we apply to these assertions the tests suggested in *Philosophical Investigations*, no such conclusion follows. All that is needed to legitimize assertions that someone means something is that

---

Wittgenstein's position here, since mathematics involves much more by way of apparently treating numbers as entities than can be covered by the simple case of counting. Perhaps some later authors can be interpreted as attempting to carry out such a project, but it is not my task to discuss these issues here.)

there be roughly specifiable circumstances under which they are legitimately assertable, and that the game of asserting them under such conditions has a role in our lives. No supposition that 'facts correspond' to those assertions is needed.

I would therefore give the following rough structure to *Philosophical Investigations* (but the breaks between parts are not sharp and to an extent are arbitrary). §§1–137 give Wittgenstein's preliminary refutation of the *Tractatus* theory of language, and suggest the rough picture he intends to put in its place. These sections come first for more than one reason. First, Wittgenstein himself once found the *Tractatus* theory natural and inevitable – Malcolm says that even in his later period he regarded it as the *only* alternative to his later work[66] – and sometimes he writes as if the reader will naturally be inclined to the *Tractatus* theory unless he personally intervenes to prevent it. Thus the initial sections contain a refutation, not only of the most basic and apparently inevitable theories of the *Tractatus* (such as meaning as stating facts), but also of many of its more special doctrines (such as that of a special realm of 'simples').[67] Wittgenstein's contrast in these initial sections between his new way of looking at matters and his old way of thinking ranges from such special views of the *Tractatus* to the nature of philosophy. This first aspect of the initial sections has, I think, been clear to most readers. Less obvious is a second aspect. The sceptical paradox is the fundamental problem of *Philosophical Investigations*. If Wittgenstein is right, we cannot begin to solve it if we remain in the grip of the natural presupposition that meaningful declarative sentences

[66] See Norman Malcolm, *Ludwig Wittgenstein: A Memoir*, with a biographical sketch by G. H. von Wright (Oxford University Press, London, 1958), p. 69.

[67] Although Wittgenstein's concern in these initial sections is primarily with his own earlier way of thinking, of course he is concerned as well with related views (the 'object and name' model of language, the picture of sentences 'as corresponding to facts', etc.) in other writers, even though these writers may have views that differ in detail from those of the *Tractatus*. He wishes to relate the discussion to larger issues as well as to his own specific views.

must purport to correspond to facts; if this is our framework, we can only conclude that sentences attributing meaning and intention are themselves meaningless. Whether or not Wittgenstein is right in thinking that the entire *Tractatus* view is a consequence of natural and apparently inevitable presuppositions, he is surely right about this fundamental part of it. The picture of correspondence-to-facts must be cleared away before we can begin with the sceptical problem.

Sections 138–242 deal with the sceptical problem and its solution. These sections – the central sections of *Philosophical Investigations* – have been the primary concern of this essay. We have not yet looked at the solution of the problem, but the astute reader already will have guessed that Wittgenstein finds a useful role in our lives for a 'language game' that licenses, under certain conditions, assertions that someone 'means such-and-such' and that his present application of a word 'accords' with what he 'meant' in the past. It turns out that this role, and these conditions, involve reference to a community. They are inapplicable to a single person considered in isolation. Thus, as we have said, Wittgenstein rejects 'private language' as early as §202.

The sections following §243 – the sections usually called 'the private language argument' – deal with the *application* of the general conclusions about language drawn in §§138–242 to the problem of sensations. The sceptical conclusion about rules, and the attendant rejection of private rules, is hard enough to swallow in general, but it seems especially unnatural in two areas. The first is mathematics, the subject of most of the preceding discussion in the present essay (and of much of Wittgenstein's in §§138–242). Do I not, in elementary mathematics, grasp rules such as that for addition, which determine all future applications? Is it not in the very nature of such rules that, once I have grasped one, I have no future choice in its application? Is not any questioning of these assertions a questioning of mathematical proof itself? And is not the grasping of a mathematical rule the solitary achievement of each mathematician independent of any interaction with a wider community? True, others may have taught me the concept of addition, but they acted only as heuristic aids to an achievement – the 'grasping of the concept' of addition – that puts me in a special relation to the addition function. Platonists have compared the grasping of a concept to a special sense, analogous to our ordinary sensory apparatus but percipient of higher entities. But the picture does not require a special Platonic theory of mathematical objects. It depends on the observation – apparently obvious on any view – that in grasping a mathematical rule I have achieved something that depends only on my own inner state, and that is immune to Cartesian doubt about the entire external material world.[68]

Now another case that seems to be an obvious counter-example to Wittgenstein's conclusion is that of a sensation, or mental image. Surely I can identify these after I have felt them, and any participation in a community is irrelevant! Because these two cases, mathematics and inner experience, seem so obviously to be counterexamples to Wittgenstein's view of rules, Wittgenstein treats each in detail. The latter case is treated in the sections following §243. The former case is treated in remarks that Wittgenstein never prepared for publication, but which are excerpted in *Remarks on the Foundations of Mathematics* and elsewhere. He thinks that only if we overcome our strong inclination to ignore his general conclusions about rules can we see these two areas rightly. For this reason, the conclusions about rules are of crucial importance both to the philosophy of mathematics and to the philosophy of mind. Although in his study of sensations in

---

[68] Although Wittgenstein's views on mathematics were undoubtedly influenced by Brouwer, it is worth noting here that Brouwer's intuitionist philosophy of mathematics is, if anything, even more solipsistic than its traditional 'Platonist' rival. According to this conception, mathematics can be idealized as the isolated activity of a single mathematician ('creating subject') whose theorems are assertions about his own mental states. The fact that mathematicians form a community is irrelevant for theoretical purposes. (Indeed, Brouwer himself is said to have held mysterious 'solipsistic' views that communication is impossible. The point would remain even if we left these aside.)

§243 onward he does not simply *cite* his general conclusions but argues this special case afresh (he does the same for mathematics elsewhere), we will only increase our difficulties in understanding an already difficult argument if we call §243 onward 'the private language argument' and study it in isolation from the preceding material. Wittgenstein had a definite plan of organization when he placed this discussion where it is.

Of course the division is not sharp. The initial 'anti-*Tractatus*' sections contain several anticipations of the 'paradox' of §§138–242,[69] and even of its solution. Sections 28–36 and sections 84–8 are examples. Even the very first section of the *Investigations* can be read, with hindsight, as anticipating the problem.[70] Nevertheless these anticipations, being cryptic allusions to the problem in the context of the problems of earlier discussion, do not fully develop the paradox and often elide the main point into other subsidiary ones.

Consider first the anticipation in sections 84–8, especially section 86, where Wittgenstein introduces the ambiguity of rules and the possibility of an infinite regress of 'rules to interpret rules'. Knowing the central problem of *Philosophical Investigations*, it is easy to see that in these sections Wittgenstein is concerned to bring out this problem, and even to allude to part of his approach to a solution (end of §87: "The sign post is in order if, in normal circumstances, it serves its purpose"). In the context, however, Wittgenstein shades his deep paradox into a much more straightforward point – that typically

---

[69] Barry Stroud emphasized this fact to me, though the responsibility for the examples and exposition in the following paragraphs is my own.

[70] See: "But how does he know where and how he is to look up the word 'red' and what he is to do with the word 'five'? – Well, I assume that he *acts* as I described. Explanations come to an end somewhere." (§1) In hindsight, this is a statement of the basic point that I follow rules 'blindly', without any justification for the choice I make. The suggestion in the section that nothing is wrong with this situation, provided that my use of 'five', 'red', etc. fits into a proper system of activities in the community, anticipates Wittgenstein's sceptical solution, as expounded below.

uses of language do not give a precise determination of their application in all cases. (See the discussion of names in §79 – "I use the name . . . without a *fixed* meaning"; of the 'chair' (?) in §80; 'Stand roughly here' in §88.) It is true, as Wittgenstein says, that his paradox shows, among other things, that every explanation of a rule could conceivably be misunderstood, and that in this respect the most apparently precise use of language does not differ from 'rough' or 'inexact', or 'open-textured' uses. Nevertheless, surely the real point of Wittgenstein's paradox is not that the rule of addition is somehow *vague*, or leaves some cases of its application undetermined. On the contrary, the word 'plus' denotes a function whose determination is *completely* precise – in this respect it does *not* resemble the vague notions expressed by 'large', 'green', and the like. The point is the sceptical problem, outlined above, that anything in my head leaves it undetermined *what* function 'plus' (as I use it) denotes (plus or quus), what 'green' denotes (green or grue), and so on. The ordinary observation, made in abstraction from any scepticism about the meaning of 'green', that the property of greenness is itself only vaguely defined for some cases, is at best distantly related. In my opinion, Wittgenstein's sceptical arguments in no way show, in this sense, that the addition function is only vaguely defined. The addition function – as Frege would emphasize – yields one precise value for each pair of numerical arguments. This much is a theorem of arithmetic. The sceptical problem indicates no vagueness in the *concept* of addition (in the way there *is* vagueness in the concept of greenness), or in the word 'plus', *granting* it its usual meaning (in the way the word 'green' *is* vague). The sceptical point is something else.[71]

[71] Though perhaps vagueness, in the ordinary sense, enters into Wittgenstein's puzzle in this way: when a teacher *introduces* such a word as 'plus' to the learner, if he does not reduce it to more 'basic', previously learned concepts, he introduces it by a finite number of examples, plus the instructions: "Go on in the same way!" The last clause may indeed be regarded as vague, in the ordinary sense, though our grasp of the most precise concept depends on it. This type of vagueness *is* intimately connected with Wittgenstein's paradox.

In the sections under discussion, Wittgenstein is arguing that *any* explanation *may* fail of its purpose: if it does not in fact fail, it may work perfectly, even if the concepts involved violate the Fregean requirement of 'sharp boundaries' (§71). See §88: "If I tell someone "Stand roughly here" may not this explanation work perfectly? And cannot every other one fail too?" At least two issues are involved here: the propriety of vagueness, of violations of the Fregean requirement (actually Wittgenstein questions whether this requirement, in an absolute sense, is well-defined); and an adumbration of the sceptical paradox of the second portion (§§138-242) of the *Investigations*. In its present context, the paradox, briefly foreshadowed, is not clearly distinguished from the other considerations about vagueness and sharp boundaries. The real development of the problem is yet to come.

Similar remarks apply to the discussion of ostensive definition in §§28–36, which is part of a larger discussion of naming, one of the important topics for the first portion (§§1–137) of the *Investigations*. Wittgenstein emphasizes that ostensive definitions are always in principle capable of being misunderstood, even the ostensive definition of a color word such as 'sepia'. How someone understands the word is exhibited in the way someone goes on, "the use that he makes of the word defined". One may go on in the right way given a purely minimal explanation, while on the other hand one may go on in another way no matter how many clarifications are added, since these too can be misunderstood (a rule for interpreting a rule again; see especially §§28–9).

Much of Wittgenstein's argument is directed against the view of a special, qualitatively unique experience of understanding the ostensive definition in the right way (§§33–6). Once again Wittgenstein's real point, here in the context of naming and ostensive definition, is the sceptical paradox. The case of ostensive definition of a color ('sepia') has a special connection with the so-called 'private language argument', as developed for sensations in §§243ff. Here too, however, the argument is adumbrated so briefly, and is so much embedded in a context of other issues, that at this stage of the argument the point can easily be lost.[72]

Yet another feature of the situation indicates how the ideas can be connected in a way that cuts across the indicated divisions of *Philosophical Investigations*. The first part (up to §137), as we have said, criticizes Wittgenstein's earlier picture of the nature of language and attempts to suggest another. Since Wittgenstein's sceptical solution of his paradox is possible only given his later conception of language and is ruled out by the earlier one, the discussion in the second part (§§138–242) is dependent on that of the first. The point to be made here is that, at the same time, the second part is important for an ultimate understanding of the first. Wittgen-

---

[72] In these sections, Wittgenstein does not cite examples like 'grue' or 'quus' but begins by emphasizing the ordinary possibilities for misunderstanding an ostensive definition. Many philosophers who have been influenced by Wittgenstein have happened also to be attracted to the idea that an act of ostension is ill defined unless it is accompanied by a sortal ('the entity I am pointing to' versus 'the color I am pointing to', 'the shape . . .', 'the table . . .', etc.). Then morals regarding naming and identity (as associated with 'sortal terms') are drawn from this fact. I have the impression that many of these philosophers would interpret Wittgenstein's §§28–9 as making the same point. (See, e.g., M. Dummett, *Frege* (Duckworth, London, 1973, xxv + 698 pp.), pp. 179–80, and frequently elsewhere.) However, it seems clear to me that the *main* point of these sections is almost the exact opposite. It should be clear from reading §29 that the idea of adding a sortal ("This *number* is called 'two'") is introduced by Wittgenstein's imaginary interlocutor. As against this, Wittgenstein replies that the point is in a sense correct, but that the original ostensive definition – without a sortal – is perfectly legitimate provided that it leads the learner to apply such a word as 'two' correctly in the future, while even if the sortal term is added, the possibility of future misapplication is not removed, since the sortal too may be interpreted incorrectly (and this problem cannot be removed by further explanations). Really there are two separable issues, as in the case of §§84–8. One issue is analogous to the one about vagueness in §§84–8: that an ostensive definition without an accompanying sortal is vague. The other, which clearly is the main point, is Wittgenstein's sceptical problem, presented here in terms of the possibility of misunderstanding an ostensive definition.

stein's earlier work had taken for granted a natural relation of interpretation between a thought in someone's mind and the 'fact' it 'depicts'. The relation was supposed to consist in an isomorphism between one fact (the fact that mental elements are arranged in a certain way) and another (the fact-in-the-world 'depicted'). Some of Wittgenstein's attack on this earlier idea is developed in the first part through a criticism of the notion, crucial to the *Tractatus* theory of isomorphism, of a unique decomposition of a complex into its 'ultimate' elements (see, for example, §§47–8). Clearly, however, the paradox of the second part of the *Investigations* constitutes a powerful critique of any idea that 'mental representations' uniquely correspond to 'facts', since it alleges that the components of such 'mental representations' do not have interpretations that can be 'read off' from them in a unique manner. So *a fortiori* there is no such unique interpretation of the mental 'sentences' containing them as 'depicting' one 'fact' or another.[73] In this way the relationship between the first and the second portions of the *Investigations* is reciprocal. In order for Wittgenstein's sceptical solution of his paradox to be intelligible, the 'realistic' or 'representational' picture of language must be undermined by another picture (in the first part). On the other hand, the paradox developed in the second part, antecedently to its solution, drives an important final nail (perhaps the crucial one) into the coffin of the representational picture.[74] No doubt this is one reason Wittgenstein introduces foreshadowings of the paradox already in the sections of the first part. But it also illustrates that the structural divisions I have indicated in *Philosophical Investigations* are not sharp. The investigation goes 'criss cross in every direction' (preface).

[73] The criticisms of the earlier ideas about 'isomorphism' are thus criticisms of a special alleged way of obtaining a unique interpretation of a mental representation. For Wittgenstein, given his earlier views, criticisms of the notion of isomorphism are thus of obvious special importance as a stage setting for his paradox. They are relatively less important as such a stage setting for someone who is not working his way out of this special *milieu*.

[74] Michael Dummett emphasized this point to me, though the responsibility for the present formulation is my own.

Wittgenstein's sceptical solution concedes to the sceptic that no 'truth conditions' or 'corresponding facts' in the world exist that make a statement like "Jones, like many of us, means addition by '+'" true. Rather we should look at how such assertions are *used*. Can this be adequate? Do we not call assertions like the one just quoted 'true' or 'false'? Can we not with propriety precede such assertions with 'It is a fact that' or 'It is not a fact that'? Wittgenstein's way with such objections is short. Like many others, Wittgenstein accepts the 'redundancy' theory of truth: to affirm that a statement is true (or presumably, to precede it with 'It is a fact that . . .') is simply to affirm the statement itself, and to say it is not true is to deny it: ('*p*' is true = *p*). However, one might object: (a) that only utterances of certain forms are called 'true' or 'false' – questions, for example, are not – and these are so called precisely because they purport to state facts; (b) that precisely the sentences that 'state facts' can occur as components of truth-functional compounds and their meaning in such compounds is hard to explain in terms of assertability conditions alone. Wittgenstein's way with this is also short. We *call* something a proposition, and hence true or false, when in our language we apply the calculus of truth functions to it. That is, it is just a primitive part of our language game, not susceptible of deeper explanation, that truth functions are applied to certain sentences. For the present expository purpose it is worth noting that the sections in which he discusses the concept of truth (§§134–7) *conclude* the preliminary sections on the *Tractatus* and immediately *precede* the discussion of the sceptical paradox. They lay the final groundwork needed for that discussion.

Finally, we can turn to Wittgenstein's sceptical solution and to the consequent argument against 'private' rules. We have to see under what circumstances attributions of meaning are made and what role these attributions play in our lives. Following Wittgenstein's exhortation not to think but to look, we will not reason *a priori* about the role such statements *ought* to play; rather we will find out what circumstances *actually*

license such assertions and what role this license *actually* plays.
It is important to realize that we are *not* looking for necessary
and sufficient conditions (truth conditions) for following a
rule, or an analysis of what such rule-following 'consists in'.
Indeed such conditions would constitute a 'straight' solution
to the sceptical problem, and have been rejected.

First, consider what is true of one person considered in
isolation. The most obvious fact is one that might have
escaped us after long contemplation of the sceptical paradox. It
holds no terrors in our daily lives; no one actually hesitates
when asked to produce an answer to an addition problem!
Almost all of us unhesitatingly produce the answer '125' when
asked for the sum of 68 and 57, without any thought to the
theoretical possibility that a quus-like rule might have been
appropriate! And we do so without justification. Of course, if
asked why we said '125', most of us will say that we added 8
and 7 to get 15, that we put down 5 and carried 1 and so on.
But then, what will we say if asked why we 'carried' as we do?
Might our past intention not have been that 'carry' meant
quarry; where to 'quarry' is . . .? The entire point of the
sceptical argument is that ultimately we reach a level where we
act without any reason in terms of which we can justify our
action. We act unhesitatingly but *blindly*.

This then is an important case of what Wittgenstein calls
speaking without 'justification' ('*Rechtfertigung*'), but not
'wrongfully' ('*zu Unrecht*').[75] It is part of our language game of
speaking of rules that a speaker may, without ultimately
giving any justification, follow his own confident inclination
that this way (say, responding '125') is the *right* way to

[75] See note 63. Note that in *Remarks on the Foundations of Mathematics*, v, §33
[vii, §40], Wittgenstein develops this point with respect to his general
problem about rules, agreement, and identity, while the parallel passage
in *Philosophical Investigations*, §289, is concerned with avowals of pain.
This illustrates again the connection of Wittgenstein's ideas on sensation
language with the general point about rules. Note also that the *RFM*
passage is embedded in a context of the philosophy of mathematics. The
connection of Wittgenstein's discussions of mathematics with his
discussions of sensations is another theme of the present essay.

respond, rather than another way (e.g. responding '5'). That is, the 'assertability conditions' that license an individual to say that, on a given occasion, he ought to follow his rule this way rather than that, are, ultimately, that he does what he is inclined to do.

The important thing about this case is that, if we confine ourselves to looking at one person alone, his psychological states and his external behavior, this is as far as we can go. We can say that he acts confidently at each application of a rule; that he says – without further justification – that the way he acts, rather than some quus-like alternative, is *the* way to respond. There are no circumstances under which we can say that, even if he inclines to say '125', he *should* have said '5', or *vice versa*. By definition, *he* is licensed to give, without further justification, the answer that strikes him as natural and inevitable. Under what circumstances can he be wrong, say, following the wrong rule? No one else by looking at his mind and behavior alone can say something like, "He is wrong if he does not accord with his own past intentions"; the whole point of the sceptical argument was that there can be no facts about him in virtue of which he accords with his intentions or not. All we can say, if we consider a single person in isolation, is that our ordinary practice licenses him to apply the rule in the way it strikes him.

But of course this is *not* our usual concept of following a rule. It is by no means the case that, just because someone thinks he is following a rule, there is no room for a judgement that he is not really doing so. Someone – a child, an individual muddled by a drug – may think he is following a rule even though he is actually acting at random, in accordance with no rule at all. Alternatively, he may, under the influence of a drug, suddenly act in accordance with a quus-like rule changing from his first intentions. If there could be no justification for anyone to say of a person of the first type that his confidence that he is following some rule is misplaced, or of a person of the second type that he is no longer in accord with the rule that he previously followed, there would be little content to our idea that a rule, or past intention, *binds* future choices. We are inclined to accept conditionals of such a rough type as, "If someone means addition by '+' then, if he remembers his past intention and wishes to conform to it, when he is queried about '68 + 57', he will answer '125'." The question is what substantive content such conditionals can have.

If our considerations so far are correct, the answer is that, if one person is considered in isolation, the notion of a rule as guiding the person who adopts it can have *no* substantive content. There are, we have seen, no truth conditions or facts in virtue of which it can be the case that he accords with his past intentions or not. As long as we regard him as following a rule 'privately', so that we pay attention to *his* justification conditions alone, all we can say is that he is licensed to follow the rule as it strikes him. This is why Wittgenstein says, "To think one is obeying a rule is not to obey a rule. Hence it is not possible to obey a rule 'privately'; otherwise thinking one was obeying a rule would be the same thing as obeying it." (§202)

The situation is very different if we widen our gaze from consideration of the rule follower alone and allow ourselves to consider him as interacting with a wider community. Others will then have justification conditions for attributing correct or incorrect rule following to the subject, and these will *not* be simply that the subject's own authority is unconditionally to be accepted. Consider the example of a small child learning addition. It is obvious that his teacher will not accept just any response from the child. On the contrary, the child must fulfill various conditions if the teacher is to ascribe to him mastery of the concept of addition. First, for small enough examples, the child must produce, almost all the time, the 'right' answer. If a child insists on the answer '7' to the query '2+3', and a '3' to '2+2', and makes various other elementary mistakes, the teacher will say to him, "You are not adding. Either you are computing another function" – I suppose he would not really talk quite this way to a child! – "or, more probably, you are as yet following no rule at all, but only giving whatever random answer enters your head." Suppose, however, the child gets almost all 'small' addition problems right. For larger computations, the child can make more mistakes than for 'small' problems, but it must get a certain number right and, when it is wrong, it must recognizably be 'trying to follow' the proper procedure, not a quus-like procedure, even though it makes mistakes. (Remember, the teacher is not judging how accurate or *adept* the child is as an adder, but whether he can be said to be following the rule for adding.) Now, what do I mean when I say that the teacher judges that, for certain cases, the pupil must give the 'right' answer? I mean that the teacher judges that the child has given the same answer that he himself would give. Similarly, when I said that the teacher, in order to judge that the child is adding, must judge that, for a problem with larger numbers, he is applying the 'right' procedure even if he comes out with a mistaken result, I mean that he judges that the child is applying the procedure he himself is inclined to apply.

Something similar is true for adults. If someone whom I judge to have been computing a normal addition function (that is, someone whom I judge to give, when he adds, the same answer I would give), suddenly gives answers according to procedures that differ bizarrely from my own, then I will judge that something must have happened to him, and that he is no longer following the rule he previously followed. If this happens to him generally, and his responses seem to me to display little discernible pattern, I will judge him probably to have gone insane.

From this we can discern rough assertability conditions for such a sentence as "Jones means addition by 'plus'." *Jones* is entitled, subject to correction by others, provisionally to say, "I mean addition by 'plus'," whenever he has the feeling of confidence – "now I can go on!" – that he can give 'correct' responses in new cases; and *he* is entitled, again provisionally and subject to correction by others, to judge a new response to be 'correct' simply because it is the response he is inclined to give. These inclinations (both Jones's general inclination that he has 'got it' and his particular inclination to give particular answers in particular addition problems) are to be regarded as primitive. They are not to be justified in terms of Jones's ability to interpret his own intentions or anything else. But Smith need *not* accept Jones's authority on these matters: *Smith will judge Jones to mean addition by 'plus' only if he judges that Jones's answers to particular addition problems agree with those he is inclined to give,* or, if they occasionally disagree, he can interpret Jones as at least following the proper procedure. (If Jones gives answers for very small problems disagreeing with those Smith is inclined to give, it will be difficult or impossible for Smith to interpret Jones as following the proper procedure. The same will hold if Jones's responses to larger problems are too bizarre to be errors in addition in the normal sense: for example, if he answers '5' to '68+57'.) If Jones consistently fails to give responses in agreement (in this broad sense) with Smith's, Smith will judge that he does not mean addition by 'plus'. Even if Jones did mean it in the past, the present deviation will justify Smith in judging that he has lapsed.

Sometimes Smith, by substituting some alternative interpretation for Jones's word 'plus', will be able to bring Jones's responses in line with his own. More often, he will be unable to do so and will be inclined to judge that Jones is not really following any rule at all. In all this, Smith's inclinations are regarded as just as primitive as Jones's. In no way does Smith test directly whether Jones may have in his head some rule agreeing with the one in Smith's head. Rather the point is that if, in enough concrete cases, Jones's inclinations agree with Smith's, Smith will judge that Jones is indeed following the rule for addition.

Of course if we were reduced to a babble of disagreement, with Smith and Jones asserting of each other that they are following the rule wrongly, while others disagreed with both and with each other, there would be little point to the practice just described. In fact, our actual community is (roughly) uniform in its practices with respect to addition. Any individual who claims to have mastered the concept of addition will be judged by the community to have done so if his particular responses agree with those of the community in enough cases, especially the simple ones (and if his 'wrong' answers are not often *bizarrely* wrong, as in '5' for '68 + 57', but seem to agree with ours in *procedure*, even when he makes a 'computational mistake'). An individual who passes such tests is admitted into the community as an adder; an individual who passes such tests in enough other cases is admitted as a normal speaker of the language and member of the community. Those who deviate are corrected and told (usually as children) that they have not grasped the concept of addition. One who is an incorrigible deviant in enough respects simply cannot participate in the life of the community and in communication.

Now Wittgenstein's general picture of language, as sketched above, requires for an account of a type of utterance not merely that we say under what conditions an utterance of that type can be made, but also what role and utility in our lives can be ascribed to the practice of making this type of utterance under such conditions. We say of someone else that he follows a certain rule when his responses agree with our own and deny it when they do not; but what is the utility of this practice? The utility is evident and can be brought out by considering again a man who buys something at the grocer's. The customer, when he deals with the grocer and asks for five apples, expects the grocer to count as he does, not according to some bizarre non-standard rule; and so, if his dealings with the grocer involve a computation, such as '68 + 57', he expects the grocer's responses to agree with his own. Indeed, he may entrust the computation to the grocer. Of course the grocer may make mistakes in addition; he may even make dishonest computations. But as long as the customer attributes to him a grasp of the concept of addition, he expects that at least the grocer will not behave bizarrely, as he would if he were to follow a quus-like rule; and one can even expect that, in many cases, he will come up with the same answer the customer would have given himself. When we pronounce that a child has mastered the rule of addition, we mean that we can entrust him to react as we do in interactions such as that just mentioned between the grocer and the customer. Our entire lives depend on countless such interactions, and on the 'game' of attributing to others the mastery of certain concepts or rules, thereby showing that we expect them to behave as we do.

This expectation is *not* infallibly fulfilled. It places a substantive restriction on the behavior of each individual, and is *not* compatible with just any behavior he may choose. (Contrast this with the case where we considered one person alone.) A deviant individual whose responses do not accord with those of the community in enough cases will not be judged, by the community, to be following its rules; he may even be judged to be a madman, following no coherent rule at all. When the community denies of someone that he is following certain rules, it excludes him from various transactions such as the one between the grocer and the customer. It indicates that it cannot rely on his behavior in such transactions.

We can restate this in terms of a device that has been common in philosophy, *inversion* of a conditional.[76] For example, it is important to our concept of causation that we accept some such conditional as: "If events of type *A* cause

---

[76] As will be seen immediately, inversion in this sense is a device for reversing priorities. William James summarized his famous theory of the emotions (*The Principles of Psychology*, Henry Holt & Co., New York, 1913, in 2 volumes; chapter 25 (vol. 2, 442–85), "The Emotions") by the assertion, ". . . the . . . rational statement is that we feel sorry because we cry . . . not that we cry . . . because we are sorry . . ." (p. 450). Many philosophies can be summed up crudely (no doubt, not really accurately) by slogans in similar form.: "We do not condemn certain acts because they are immoral; they are immoral because we condemn them." "We do not accept the law of contradiction because it is a necessary truth; it is a necessary truth because we accept it (by convention)." "Fire and heat are not constantly conjoined because fire causes heat; fire causes heat because they are constantly conjoined" (Hume). "We do not all say

events of type B, and if an event e of type A occurs, then an event e' of type B must follow." So put, it appears that acceptance of the conditional commits us to a belief in a nexus so that, given that the causal connection between event types obtains, the occurrence of the first event e necessitates (by fulfilling the antecedent of the conditional), that an event e' of type B must obtain. Humeans, of course, deny the existence of such a nexus; how do they read the conditional? Essentially they concentrate on the assertability conditions of a contrapositive form of the conditional. It is not that any antecedent conditions necessitate that some event e' must take place; rather the conditional commits us, whenever we know that an event e of type A occurs and is not followed by an event of type B, to deny that there is a causal connection between the two event types. If we did make such a claim, we must now withdraw it. Although a conditional is equivalent to its contrapositive, concentration on the contrapositive reverses our priorities. Instead of seeing causal connections as primary, from which observed regularities 'flow', the Humean instead sees the regularity as primary, and – looking at the matter contrapositively – observes that we withdraw a causal hypothesis when the corresponding regularity has a definite counter-instance.

A similar inversion is used in the present instance. It is essential to our concept of a rule that we maintain some such conditional as "If Jones means addition by '$+$', then if he is asked for '$68+57$', he will reply '125'." (Actually many clauses should be added to the antecedent to make it strictly correct, but for present purposes let us leave it in this rough form.) As in the causal case, the conditional as stated makes it appear that

---

$12+7=19$ and the like because we all grasp the concept of addition; we say we all grasp the concept of addition because we all say $12+7=19$ and the like" (Wittgenstein).

The device of inversion of a conditional in the text achieves the effect of reversing priorities in a way congenial to such slogans. Speaking for myself, I am suspicious of philosophical positions of the types illustrated by the slogans, whether or not they are so crudely put.

some mental state obtains in Jones that guarantees his performance of particular additions such as '68 + 57' – just what the sceptical argument denies. Wittgenstein's picture of the true situation concentrates on the contrapositive, and on justification conditions. If Jones does *not* come out with '125' when asked about '68 + 57', we cannot assert that he means addition by '+'. Actually, of course, this is not strictly true, because our formulation of the conditional is overly loose; other conditions must be added to the antecedent to make it true. As the conditional is stated, not even the possibility of computational error is taken into account, and there are many complications not easily spelled out. The fact remains that if we ascribe to Jones the conventional concept of addition, we do not expect him to exhibit a pattern of bizarre, quus-like behavior. By such a conditional we do not mean, on the Wittgensteinian view, that any state of Jones guarantees his correct behavior. Rather by asserting such a conditional we commit ourselves, if in the future Jones behaves bizarrely enough (and on enough occasions), no longer to persist in our assertion that he is following the conventional rule of addition.

The rough conditional thus expresses a restriction on the community's game of attributing to one of its members the grasping of a certain concept: if the individual in question no longer conforms to what the community would do in these circumstances, the community can no longer attribute the concept to him. Even though, when we play this game and attribute concepts to individuals, we depict no special 'state' of their minds, we do something of importance. We take them provisionally into the community, as long as further deviant behavior does not exclude them. In practice, such deviant behavior rarely occurs.

It is, then, in such a description of the game of concept attribution that Wittgenstein's sceptical solution consists. It provides both conditions under which we are justified in attributing concepts to others and an account of the utility of this game in our lives. In terms of this account we can discuss briefly three of Wittgenstein's key concepts.

First, *agreement*. The entire 'game' we have described – that the community attributes a concept to an individual so long as he exhibits sufficient conformity, under test circumstances, to the behavior of the community – would lose its point outside a community that generally agrees in its practices. If one person, when asked to compute '68 + 57' answered '125', another '5', and another '13', if there was no general agreement in the community responses, the game of attributing concepts to individuals – as we have described it – could not exist. In fact of course there is considerable agreement, and deviant quus-like behavior occurs rarely. Mistakes and disagreements do occur, but these are another matter. The fact is that, extreme cases of uneducability or insanity aside, almost all of us, after sufficient training, respond with roughly the same procedures to concrete addition problems. We respond unhesitatingly to such problems as '68 + 57', regarding our procedure as the only comprehensible one (see, e.g., §§219, 231, 238), and we *agree* in the unhesitating responses we make. On Wittgenstein's conception, such agreement is essential for our game of ascribing rules and concepts to each other (see §240).

The set of responses in which we agree, and the way they interweave with our activities, is our *form of life*. Beings who agreed in consistently giving bizarre quus-like responses would share in another form of life. By definition, such another form of life would be bizarre and incomprehensible to us. ("If a lion could talk, we could not understand him" (p. 223).) However, if we can imagine the abstract possibility of another form of life (and no *a priori* argument would seem to exclude it), the members of a community sharing such a quus-like form of life could play the game of attributing rules and concepts to each other as we do. Someone would be said, in such a community, to follow a rule, as long as he agrees in his responses with the (*quus*-like) responses produced by the members of *that* community. Wittgenstein stresses the importance of agreement, and of a shared form of life, for his solution to his sceptical problem in the concluding paragraphs of the central section of *Philosophical Investigations* (§§240–2; see also the discussion of agreement on pp. 225–7).

On Wittgenstein's conception, a certain type of traditional – and overwhelmingly natural – explanation of our shared form of life is excluded. We cannot say that we all respond as we do to '68 + 57' *because* we all grasp the concept of addition in the same way, that we share common responses to particular addition problems *because* we share a common concept of addition. (Frege, for example, would have endorsed such an explanation, but one hardly needs to be a philosopher to find it obvious and natural.) For Wittgenstein, an 'explanation' of this kind ignores his treatment of the sceptical paradox and its solution. There is no objective fact – that we all mean addition by ' + ', or even that a given individual does – that explains our agreement in particular cases. Rather our license to say of each other that we mean addition by ' + ' is part of a 'language game' that sustains itself only because of the brute fact that we generally agree. (Nothing about 'grasping concepts' guarantees that it will not break down tomorrow.) The rough uniformities in our arithmetical behavior may or may not some day be given an explanation on the neurophysiological level, but such an explanation is not here in question.[77] Note again the analogy with the Humean case. Naively, we may wish to explain the observed concomitance of fire and heat by a causal, heat-producing, 'power' in the fire. The Humean alleges that any such use of causal powers to explain the regularity is meaningless. Rather we play a language game that allows us to attribute such a causal power to the fire as

[77] Modern transformational linguistics, inasmuch as it explains all my specific utterances by my 'grasp' of syntactic and semantic rules generating infinitely many sentences with their interpretation, seems to give an explanation of the type Wittgenstein would not permit. For the explanation is *not* in terms of my actual 'performance' as a finite (and fallible) device. It is not a purely causal (neurophysiological) explanation in the sense explained in the text; see note 22 above. On the other hand, some aspects of Chomsky's views are very congenial to Wittgenstein's conception. In particular, according to Chomsky, highly species-specific constraints – a 'form of life' – lead a child to project, on the basis of exposure to a limited corpus of sentences, a variety of new sentences for new situations. There is no *a priori* inevitability in the child's going on in the way he does, other than that this is what the species does. As was already said in note 22, the matter deserves a more extended discussion.

long as the regularity holds up. The regularity must be taken as a brute fact. So too for Wittgenstein (p. 226): "What has to be accepted, the given, is . . . *forms of life.*"[78]

Finally, _criteria._ The exact interpretation and exegesis of Wittgenstein's concept of a criterion has been the subject of much discussion among students of Wittgenstein's later work. Criteria play a fundamental role in Wittgenstein's philosophy of mind: "An 'inner process' stands in need of outward criteria" (§580). Often the necessity for criteria for mental concepts has been taken, both by advocates and critics of Wittgenstein's philosophy of mind, as a fundamental *premise* of

---

[78] Can we imagine forms of life other than our own, that is, can we imagine creatures who follow rules in bizarre quus-like ways? It seems to me that there may be a certain tension in Wittgenstein's philosophy here. On the one hand, it would seem that Wittgenstein's paradox argues that there is no *a priori* reason why a creature could not follow a quus-like rule, and thus in this sense we ought to regard such creatures as conceivable. On the other hand, it is supposed to be part of our very form of life that we find it natural and, indeed, inevitable that we follow the rule for addition in the particular way that we do. (See §231: "But surely you can see . . .?" That is just the characteristic expression of someone who is under the compulsion of a rule.") But then it seems that we should be unable to understand 'from the inside' (cf. the notion of '*Verstehen*' in various German writers) how any creature could follow a quus-like rule. We could describe such behavior extensionally and behavioristically, but we would be unable to find it intelligible how the creature finds it natural to behave in this way. This consequence does, indeed, seem to go with Wittgenstein's conception of the matter.

Of course we can define the quus function, introduce a symbol for it, and follow the appropriate rule for computing its values. I have done so in this very essay. What it seems may be unintelligible to us is how an intelligent creature could get the very training we have for the addition function, and yet grasp the appropriate function in a quus-like way. If such a possibility were really completely intelligible to us, would we find it so inevitable to apply the plus function as we do? Yet this inevitability is an essential part of Wittgenstein's own solution to his problem.

The point is even stronger with respect to a term like 'green'. Can we grasp how someone could be presented with a number of green objects, and be told to apply the term 'green' just to 'things like these', and yet apply the term learnt as if it meant 'grue'? It would seem that if we find our own continuation to be inevitable, in some sense we cannot.

his private language argument. Critics have sometimes argued that it constitutes an undefended and indefensible verificationist assumption. Some advocates respond that if it is a verificationist premise of some sort, that form of verificationism is clearly correct.

It is not my present purpose to enter into the finer exegetical points involved in Wittgenstein's notion of a criterion,[79] but rather to sketch the role of the notion in the picture we have been developing. Wittgenstein's sceptical solution to his problem depends on agreement, and on checkability – on one person's ability to test whether another uses a term as he does. In our own form of life, how does this agreement come about? In the case of a term like 'table', the situation, at least in elementary cases, is simple. A child who says "table" or "That's a table" when adults see a table in the area (and does not do so otherwise) is said to have mastered the term 'table': he says "That's a table", based on his observation, in agreement with the usage of adults, based on their observation. That is, they say, "That's a table" under like circumstances, and confirm the correctness of the child's utterances.

How does agreement emerge in the case of a term for a sensation, say 'pain'? It is not as simple as the case of 'table'. When will adults attribute to a child mastery of the avowal "I am in pain"?[80] The child, if he learns the avowal correctly, will utter it when he feels pain and not otherwise. By analogy with the case of 'table', it would appear that the adult should endorse this utterance if he, the adult, feels (his own? the child's?) pain. Of course we know that this is not the case. Rather the adult will endorse the child's avowal if the child's behavior (crying, agitated motion, etc.) and, perhaps, the

---

[79] One detailed attempt to enter into such issues is Rogers Albritton, "On Wittgenstein's Use of the Term 'Criterion'," in Pitcher (ed.), *Wittgenstein: The Philosophical Investigations*, pp. 231–50, reprinted with a new postscript from *The Journal of Philosophy*, vol. 56 (1959), pp. 845–57.

[80] Following recent (perhaps not wholly attractive) philosophical usage, I call a first person assertion that the speaker has a certain sensation (e.g. "I am in pain") an 'avowal'.

external circumstances surrounding the child, indicate that he is in pain. If a child generally avows pain under such appropriate behavioral and external circumstances and generally does not do so otherwise, the adult will say of him that he has mastered the avowal, "I am in pain."

Since, in the case of discourse on pain and other sensations, the adult's confirmation whether he agrees with the child's avowal is based on the adult's observation of the child's behavior and circumstances, the fact that such behavior and circumstances characteristic of pain exist is essential in this case to the working of Wittgenstein's sceptical solution. This, then, is what is meant by the remark, "An 'inner process' stands in need of outward criteria." Roughly speaking, outward criteria for an inner process are circumstances, observable in the behavior of an individual, which, when present, would lead others to agree with his avowals. If the individual generally makes his avowals under the right such circumstances, others will say of him that he has mastered the appropriate expression ("I am in pain," "I feel itchy," etc.). We have seen that it is part of Wittgenstein's *general* view of the workings of *all* our expressions attributing concepts that others can confirm whether a subject's responses agree with their own. The present considerations simply spell out the form this confirmation and agreement take in the case of avowals.

It should then be clear that the demand for 'outward criteria' is no verificationist or behaviorist *premise* that Wittgenstein takes for granted in his 'private language argument'. If anything, it is *deduced*, in a sense of deduction akin to Kant's.[81]

---

[81] See also the postscript below, note 5.

    Note that it would be difficult to imagine how a causal neurophysiological explanation of the uniformities in our attributions of sensations to others (of the type mentioned on p. 97 above) could be possible if there were no 'outward' manifestations of sensations. For – except perhaps in minute or subliminal ways – the sensations of one person are causally connected to those of others only by the mediation of external signs and behavior. (I assume that 'extrasensory perception' is not in question here.) If the mediating external correlates did not exist, how could the fact

A sceptical problem is posed, and a sceptical solution to that problem is given. The solution turns on the idea that each person who claims to be following a rule can be checked by others. Others in the community can check whether the putative rule follower is or is not giving particular responses that they endorse, that agree with their own. The way they check this is, in general, a primitive part of the language game;[82] it need not operate the way it does in the case of 'table'.

----

that others agree in their judgement that a given individual has a certain sensation have a causal explanation? Causally, it would have to be a coincidence. (Similarly for the uniformities in our mathematical judgements mentioned on pp. 105–6 below.)

However, Wittgenstein does not himself seem to be particularly concerned with neurophysiological explanations of such uniformities but wants to take them as 'protophenomena' (§§654–5), where the search for an explanation is a mistake. Although I do not think such remarks are meant to rule out causal neurophysiological explanations of the uniformities, it does not appear, philosophically, that Wittgenstein wishes to *rely* on the concept of such neurophysiological explanations either.

Obviously it *would* be incompatible with Wittgenstein's argument to seek to 'explain' our agreement on whether a given individual is in pain in terms of our uniform 'grasp' of the concept of *pain behavior*. The fact that we agree on whether a given individual is, or is not, say, groaning, comes within the purview of Wittgenstein's sceptical arguments as much as does any other case of 'following a rule'. The causal argument sketched above is something else. (Although I have tried to avoid invoking such an argument explicitly in my discussion of 'outward criteria' in the text, since – as I said – Wittgenstein does not seem to wish to rely on such considerations, it has sometimes seemed to me that such a causal argument is implicitly involved if it is to be argued that the criteria we actually use are *essential* to our 'language game' of attributing sensations.)

My discussion in this footnote and the preceding text was influenced by a question of G. E. M. Anscombe.

82 The criterion by which others judge whether a person is obeying a rule in a given instance cannot simply be his sincere inclination to say that he is; otherwise there would be no distinction between his thinking he is obeying the rule and his really obeying it (§202), and whatever he thinks is right will be right (§258). However, *after* the community judges (based on the original criteria) that he has mastered the appropriate rule, the community may (for certain rules) take the subject's sincere claim to follow it in this instance as in itself a new criterion for the correctness of

'Outward criteria' for sensations such as pain are simply the way this general requirement of our game of attributing concepts to others works out in the special case of sensations. [83]

___

his claim, without applying the original criteria. According to Wittgenstein, we do this in the case of 'I am in pain.' In the case of 'I dreamt', the terminology is originally taught to a subject who wakes up reporting certain experiences. We judge that he has mastered the rule for 'I dreamt' if he prefaces it to reports of experiences he says he had the night before. After we judge that he has mastered the language, we take 'I dreamt that such-and-such' as in itself a criterion for correctness. In both cases of 'I am in pain' and 'I dreamt', the first person utterance is new behavior that replaces the behavior that constituted the old criterion.

Reports of after-images or hallucinations are similar. We judge that someone has mastered 'I see something red' if he ordinarily utters it only when something red is present. Once we judge, however, that he has mastered this bit of language, we will accept his utterance that he sees red even when we think nothing red is present. Then we will say that he is suffering from an illusion, a hallucination, an after-image, or the like.

[83] One delicate point regarding sensations, and about 'criteria', ought to be noted. Wittgenstein often seems to be taken to suppose that for any type of sensation, there is an appropriate 'natural expression' of that sensation type ('pain behavior' for pain). The 'natural expression' is to be externally observable behavior 'expressing' the sensation other than, and prior to, the subject's verbal avowal that he has the sensation. If the theory of §244 that first person sensation avowals are verbal replacements for a 'primitive natural expression' of a sensation has the generality it appears to have, it would follow that Wittgenstein holds that such a 'primitive natural expression' must always exist if the first person avowal is to be meaningful. The impression is reinforced by other passages such as §§256–7. Further, the presentation of the private language argument in the present essay argues that for each rule I follow there must be a criterion – other than simply what I say – by which another will judge that I am following the rule correctly. Applied to sensations, this seems to mean that there must be some 'natural expression', or at any rate some external circumstances other than my mere inclination to say that this is the same sensation again, in virtue of which someone else can judge whether the sensation is present, and hence whether I have mastered the sensation term correctly. So the picture would be that to each statement of the form "I have sensation S" there must be an 'outward criterion' associated with S, other than the mere avowal itself, by which others recognize the presence or absence of S.

Not only professed followers of Wittgenstein but many who think of themselves as opponents (or, at least, not followers) of Wittgenstein, seem to think that something of this kind is true. That is to say, many philosophical programs seem to suppose that all sensation types are associated with some characteristic external phenomena (behavior, causes). In this essay I have largely suppressed my own views, which are by no means always in agreement with Wittgenstein's. However, I will permit myself to remark here that any view that supposes that, in this sense, an inner process always has 'outward criteria', seems to me probably to be *empirically* false. It seems to me that we have sensations or sensation *qualia* that we can perfectly well identify but that have no 'natural' external manifestations; an observer cannot tell in any way whether an individual has them unless that individual avows them. Perhaps a more liberal interpretation of the private language argument – which *may* be compatible with what Wittgenstein intended – would allow that a speaker might introduce some sensation terms with no 'outward criteria' for the associated sensations beyond his own sincere avowal of them. (Hence these avowals do not 'replace' any 'natural expressions' of the sensation(s), for there are none.) There will be no way anyone else will be in any position to check such a speaker, or to agree or disagree with him. (No matter what many Wittgensteinians – or Wittgenstein – would infer here, this does not in itself entail that his avowals are regarded as infallible, nor need it in itself mean that there could not later come to be ways of checking his avowals.) However, the language of the speaker, even his language of sensations, will not have the objectionable form of a 'private language', one in which anything he calls 'right' is right. The speaker can demonstrate, for many sensations that do have 'public criteria', that he has mastered the appropriate terminology for identifying these sensations. If we agree with his responses in enough cases of various sensations, we say of him that he has mastered 'sensation language'. All this, so far, is subject to external correction. But it is a primitive part of our language game of sensations that, if an individual has satisfied criteria for a mastery of sensation language in general, we then respect his claim to have identified a new type of sensation even if the sensation is correlated with nothing publicly observable. Then the only 'public criterion' for such an avowal will be the sincere avowal itself.

How does the view sketched here liberalize the private language argument as developed in the text? In the text we argued that *for each particular rule*, if conditionals of the form "If Jones follows the rule, in this instance he will . . ." are to have any point, they must be contraposed. If the community finds that in this instance Jones is not doing . . ., he is not following the rule. Only in this 'inverted' way does the notion of my behavior as 'guided' by the rule make sense. Thus for each rule there must be an 'external check' on whether I am following it in a given instance. Perhaps §202 should be taken to assert this. But this means the

It is not my purpose here to enter in detail into the exegesis of Wittgenstein's attack on an 'object and designation' model for sensation language (§293). I am not, in fact, sure that I fully

community must have a way of telling ('criterion') whether it is being followed in a given instance, which it uses to judge the speaker's mastery of the rule. This criterion cannot be simply the speaker's own sincere inclination to follow the rule a certain way – otherwise, the conditional has no content. This condition seems to be satisfied even in those cases where, *after* the community is satisfied that the speaker has mastered the language, it lets the speaker's sincere utterance be a (or *the*) criterion for their correctness. (See note 82.) In contrast, the liberal version allows that once a speaker, judged by criteria for mastery of various rules, is accepted into the community, there should be some rules where there is no way for others to check his mastery, but where that mastery is simply presumed on the basis of his membership in the community. This is simply a primitive feature of the language game. Why should Wittgenstein not allow language games like this?

I regret that I have discussed this matter so briefly in a note. I had thought at one time to expound the 'liberal' view sketched here as the 'official' Wittgensteinian doctrine, which would have facilitated an exposition at greater length in the text. Certainly it is the one Wittgenstein should have adopted in accordance with the slogan "Don't think, look!", and it really is compatible with his attack on private language. On writing the final version of this essay, however, I came to worry that passages such as §244 and §§256–7 are highly misleading unless Wittgenstein holds something stronger.

(After writing the preceding, I found that Malcolm, in his *Thought and Knowledge* (Cornell University Press, Ithaca and London, 1977, 218 pp.), writes (p. 101), "philosophers sometimes read Wittgenstein's insistence on there being a conceptual link between statements of sensation and the primitive, natural, expressions of sensation in human behavior, as implying that there is a natural nonverbal, behavioral counterpart of *every* statement of sensation. Wittgenstein did not mean this, and it is obviously not true." I agree that it is not true. I think it is not true even for simple avowals invoking what we might call 'names' of sensations. ("I have sensation S.") But – what is a separate question – did Wittgenstein mean this? It seems to me that even some of Malcolm's own previous expositions of Wittgenstein have given (unintentionally?) the impression that he did, at least for simple avowals invoking 'names of sensations'. I myself have vacillated on the question. Whether or not Wittgenstein meant this, I do think that the essence of his doctrines can be captured without commitment to such a strong claim.)

understand it. But it seems likely that it relates to one aspect of our present considerations. The model of the way agreement operates with respect to a word like 'table' (perhaps a paradigm of 'object and designation') is a very simple one: the child says "Table!" when he sees that a table is present and the adult agrees if he also sees that a table is present. It is tempting to suppose that this model ought to be a general one, and that if it does not apply to the case of 'pain' we must conclude that in some sense the adult can never really confirm the correctness of the child's use of "I am in pain." Wittgenstein's suggestion is that there cannot and need not be such a demand based on generalizing the use of 'table'. No *a priori* paradigm of the way concepts ought to be applied governs all forms of life, or even our own form of life. Our game of attributing concepts to others depends on agreement. It so happens that in the case of ascribing sensation language, this agreement operates in part through 'outward criteria' for first person avowals. No further 'justification' or 'explanation' for this procedure is required; this simply is *given* as how we achieve agreement here. The important role played in our lives by the practice of attributing sensation concepts to others is evident. If I attribute mastery of the term 'pain' to someone, his sincere utterance of "I am in pain," even without other signs of pain, is sufficient to induce me to feel pity for him, attempt to aid him, and the like (or, if I am a sadist, for the opposite); and similarly in other cases.

Compare the case of mathematics. Mathematical statements are generally not about palpable entities: if they are indeed to be regarded as about 'entities', these 'entities' are generally suprasensible, eternal objects. And often mathematical statements are about the infinite. Even such an elementary mathematical truth as that any two integers have a unique sum (perhaps implicitly accepted by everyone who has mastered the concept of addition, and in any case, explicitly accepted by people with elementary sophistication as a basic property of that concept) is an assertion about infinitely many instances. All the more so is this true of the 'commutative' law, that $x+y=y+x$ for all x and y. Yet how does agreement operate in the case of mathematics? How do we judge of someone else that he has mastered various mathematical concepts? Our judgement, as usual, stems from the fact that he agrees with us in enough particular cases of mathematical judgements (and that, even if he disagrees, we are operating with a common procedure). We do not compare his mind with some suprasensible, infinite reality: we have seen through the sceptical paradox that this is of no help if we ask, say, whether he has mastered the concept of addition. Rather we check his observable responses to particular addition problems to see if his responses agree with ours. In more sophisticated mathematical areas, he and we accept various mathematical statements on the basis of proof; and among the conditions we require for attributing to him the mastery of our mathematical concepts is his general agreement with us on what he regards as proof. Here 'proofs' are not abstract objects laid up in a mathematical heaven (say, lengthy proofs in a formal system such as *Principia*). They are visible (or audible or palpable), concrete phenomena – marks or diagrams on paper, intelligible utterances. Proofs in this sense are not only finite objects; they are also short and clear enough for me to be able to judge of another person's proof whether I too would regard it as proof. That is why Wittgenstein emphasizes that proof must be *surveyable*. It must be surveyable if it is to be usable as a basis for agreement in judgements.

This parallel illuminates Wittgenstein's remark that "Finitism and behaviorism are quite similar trends. Both say, but surely, all we have here is . . . Both deny the existence of something, both with a view to escaping from a confusion." (*Remarks on the Foundations of Mathematics*, p. 63 [II, §61]) How are the two trends 'quite similar'? The finitist realizes that although mathematical statements and concepts may be about the infinite (e.g., to grasp the '+' function is to grasp an infinite table), the criteria for attributing such functions to others must be 'finite', indeed 'surveyable' – for example, we attribute mastery of the concept of addition to a child on the basis of his agreement with us on a finite number of instances of the addition table. Similarly, though sensation language may be about 'inner' states, the behaviorist correctly affirms that attribution to others of sensation concepts rests on publicly observable (and thus on behavioral) criteria. Further, the finitist and the behaviorist are right when they deny that the relation of the infinitary mathematical or inner psychological language to its 'finite' or 'outward' criteria is an adventitious product of human frailty, one that an account of the 'essence' of mathematical or sensation language would dispense with. Mathematical finitists and psychological behaviorists, however, make parallel unnecessary moves when they deny the legitimacy of talk of infinite mathematical objects or inner states. Behaviorists either condemn talk of mental states as meaningless or illegitimate, or attempt to define it in terms of behavior. Finitists similarly regard the infinitistic part of mathematics as meaningless. Such opinions are misguided: they are attempts to repudiate our ordinary language game. In this game we are allowed, for certain purposes, to assert statements about 'inner' states or mathematical functions under certain circumstances. Although the criteria for judging that such statements are legitimately introduced are indeed behavioral (or finite), finite or behavioral statements cannot replace their role in our language as we use it.

Let me, then, summarize the 'private language argument' as it is presented in this essay. (1) We all suppose that our language expresses concepts – 'pain', 'plus', 'red' – in such a way that, once I 'grasp' the concept, all future applications of it are determined (in the sense of being uniquely *justified* by the concept grasped). In fact, it seems that no matter what is in my mind at a given time, I am free in the future to interpret it in different ways – for example, I could follow the sceptic and interpret 'plus' as 'quus'. In particular, this point applies if I direct my attention to a sensation and name it; nothing I have done determines future applications (in the justificatory sense above). Wittgenstein's scepticism about the determination of future usage by the past contents of my mind is analogous to

Hume's scepticism about the determination of the future by the past (causally and inferentially). (2) The paradox can be resolved only by a 'sceptical solution of these doubts', in Hume's classic sense. This means that we must give up the attempt to find any fact about me in virtue of which I mean 'plus' rather than 'quus', and must then go on in a certain way. Instead we must consider how we actually use: (i) the categorical assertion that an individual is following a given rule (that he means addition by 'plus'); (ii) the conditional assertion that "if an individual follows such-and-such a rule, he must do so-and-so on a given occasion" (e.g., "if he means addition by '+', his answer to '68 + 57' should be '125'"). That is to say, we must look at the circumstances under which these assertions are introduced into discourse, and their role and utility in our lives. (3) As long as we consider a single individual in isolation, all we can say is this: An individual often does have the experience of being confident that he has 'got' a certain rule (sometimes that he has grasped it 'in a flash'). It is an empirical fact that, after that experience, individuals often are disposed to give responses in concrete cases with complete confidence that proceeding this way is 'what was intended'. We cannot, however, get any further in explaining on this basis the use of the conditionals in (ii) above. Of course, dispositionally speaking, the subject is indeed determined to respond in a certain way, say, to a given addition problem. Such a disposition, together with the appropriate 'feeling of confidence', could be present, however, even if he were not really following a rule at all, or even if he were doing the 'wrong' thing. The justificatory element of our use of conditionals such as (ii) is unexplained. (4) If we take into account the fact that the individual is in a community, the picture changes and the role of (i) and (ii) above becomes apparent. When the community accepts a particular conditional (ii), it accepts its *contraposed* form: the failure of an individual to come up with the particular responses the community regards as right leads the community to suppose that he is not following the rule. On the other hand, if an individual passes enough tests, the community (endorsing assertions of the form (i)) accepts him as a rule follower, thus enabling him to engage in certain types of interactions with them that depend on their reliance on his responses. Note that this solution explains how the assertions in (i) and (ii) are introduced into language; it does *not* give conditions for these statements to be true. (5) The success of the practices in (3) depends on the brute empirical fact that we agree with each other in our responses. Given the sceptical argument in (1), this success cannot be explained by 'the fact that we all grasp the same concepts'. (6) Just as Hume thought he had demonstrated that the causal relation between two events is unintelligible unless they are subsumed under a regularity, so Wittgenstein thought that the considerations in (2) and (3) above showed that all talk of an individual following rules has reference to him as a member of a community, as in (3). In particular, for the conditionals of type (ii) to make sense, the community must be able to judge whether an individual is indeed following a given rule in particular applications, i.e. whether his responses agree with their own. In the case of avowals of sensations, the way the community makes this judgement is by observing the individual's behavior and surrounding circumstances.

A few concluding points regarding the argument ought to be noted. First, following §243, a 'private language' is usually defined as a language that is logically impossible for anyone else to understand. The private language argument is taken to argue against the possibility of a private language in this sense. This conception is not in error, but it seems to me that the emphasis is somewhat misplaced. What is really denied is what might be called the 'private model' of rule following, that the notion of a person following a given rule is to be analyzed simply in terms of facts about the rule follower and the rule follower alone, without reference to his membership in a wider community. (In the same way, what Hume denies is the private model of causation: that whether one event causes another is a matter of the relation between these two events alone, without reference to their subsumption under larger event types.) The impossibility of a private language in the sense just defined does indeed follow from the incorrectness of the private model for language and rules, since the rule following in a 'private language' could only be analyzed by a private model, but the incorrectness of the private model is more basic, since it applies to all rules. I take all this to be the point of §202.

Does this mean that Robinson Crusoe, isolated on an island, cannot be said to follow any rules, no matter what he does?[84] I do not see that this follows. What does follow is that *if* we think of Crusoe as following rules, we are taking him into our community and applying our criteria for rule following to him.[85] The falsity of the private model need not mean that a *physically isolated* individual cannot be said to follow rules; rather that an individual, *considered in isolation* (whether or not he is physically isolated), cannot be said to do so. Remember that Wittgenstein's theory is one of assertability conditions. Our community can assert of any individual that he follows a rule if he passes the tests for rule following applied to any member of the community.

Finally, the point just made in the last paragraph, that

---

[84] See the well-known exchange between A. J. Ayer and Rush Rhees under the title "Can there be a Private Language?" (see note 47). Both participants in the exchange assume that the 'private language argument' excludes Crusoe from language. Ayer takes this alleged fact to be fatal to Wittgenstein's argument, while Rhees takes it to be fatal to Crusoe's language. Others, pointing out that a 'private language' is one that others *cannot* understand (see the preceding paragraph in the text), see no reason to think that the 'private language argument' has anything to do with Crusoe (as long as we could understand his language). My own view of the matter, as explained very briefly in the text, differs somewhat from all these opinions.

[85] If Wittgenstein would have any problem with Crusoe, perhaps the problem would be whether we have any 'right' to take him into our community in this way, and attribute our rules to him. See Wittgenstein's discussion of a somewhat similar question in §§199–200, and his conclusion, "Should we still be inclined to say they were playing a game? What right would one have to say so?"

Wittgenstein's theory is one of assertability conditions, deserves emphasis. Wittgenstein's theory should not be confused with a theory that, for any *m* and *n*, the value of the function we mean by 'plus', *is* (by definition) the value that (nearly) all the linguistic community would give as the answer. Such a theory would be a theory of the *truth* conditions of such assertions as "By 'plus' we mean such-and-such a function," or "By 'plus' we mean a function, which, when applied to 68 and 57 as arguments, yields 125 as value." (An infinite, exhaustive totality of specific conditions of the second form would determine which function was meant, and hence would determine a condition of the first form.) The theory would assert that 125 is the value of the function meant for given arguments, if and only if '125' is the response nearly everyone would give, given these arguments. Thus the theory would be a social, or community-wide, version of the dispositional theory, and would be open to at least some of the same criticisms as the original form. I take Wittgenstein to deny that he holds such a view, for example, in *Remarks on the Foundations of Mathematics*, v, §33 [vii, §40] : "Does this mean, e.g., that the definition of the same would be this: same is what all or most human beings . . . take for the same?–Of course not."[86] (See also *Philosophical Investigations*, p. 226, "Certainly the propositions, "Human beings believe that twice two is four" and "Twice two is four" do not mean the same"; and see also §§240–1.) One must bear firmly in mind that Wittgenstein has no theory of truth conditions – necessary and sufficient conditions – for the correctness of one response rather than another to a new addition problem. Rather he simply points out that each of us *automatically* calculates new addition problems (without feeling the need to check with the community whether our procedure is proper); that the community feels entitled to correct a deviant calculation; that

[86] Although, in the passage in question, Wittgenstein is speaking of a particular language game of bringing something else and bringing the same, it is clear in context that it is meant to illustrate his general problem about rules. The entire passage is worth reading for the present issue.

in practice such deviation is rare, and so on. Wittgenstein thinks that these observations about sufficent conditions for justified assertion are enough to illuminate the role and utility in our lives of assertion about meaning and determination of new answers. What follows from these assertability conditions is *not* that the answer everyone gives to an addition problem is, by definition, the correct one, but rather the platitude that, if everyone agrees upon a certain answer, then no one will feel justified in calling the answer wrong.[87]

Obviously there are countless relevant aspects of Wittgenstein's philosophy of mind that I have not discussed.[88] About some aspects I am not clear, and others have been left untouched because of the limits of this essay.[89] In particular, I

[87] See note added in proof, p. 146.

[88] One question goes in the opposite direction from note 87 (p. 146). As members of the community correct each other, might a given individual correct himself? Some question such as this was prominent in earlier discussions of verificationist versions of the private language argument. Indeed, in the absence of Wittgenstein's sceptical paradox, it would appear that an individual remembers his own 'intentions' and can use one memory of these intentions to correct another mistaken memory. In the presence of the paradox, any such 'naive' ideas are meaningless. Ultimately, an individual may simply have conflicting brute inclinations, while the upshot of the matter depends on his will alone. The situation is not analogous to the case of the community, where distinct individuals have distinct and independent wills, and where, when an individual is accepted into the community, others judge that they can rely on his response (as was described in the text above). No corresponding relation between an individual and himself has the same utility. Wittgenstein may be indicating something like this in §268.

[89] I might mention that, in addition to the Humean analogy emphasized in this essay, it has struck me that there is perhaps a certain analogy between Wittgenstein's private language argument and Ludwig von Mises's celebrated argument concerning economic calculation under socialism. (See e.g., his *Human Action* (2nd ed., Yale University Press, New Haven, 1963 xix+907 pp.), chapter 26, pp. 698–715, for one statement.) According to Mises, a rational economic calculator (say, the manager of an industrial plant) who wishes to choose the most efficient means to achieve given ends must compare alternative courses of action for cost effectiveness. To do this, he needs an array of prices (e.g. of raw materials, or machinery) set by *others*. If *one* agency set *all* prices, it could

have not discussed numerous issues arising out of the paragraphs *following* §243 that are usually called the 'private language argument', nor have I really discussed Wittgenstein's attendant positive account of the nature of sensation language and of the attribution of psychological states. Nevertheless, I do think that the basic 'private language argument' precedes these passages, and that only with an understanding of this argument can we begin to comprehend or consider what follows. That was the task undertaken in this essay.

---

have no rational basis to choose between alternative courses of action. (Whatever seemed to it to be right would be right, so one cannot talk about right.) I do not know whether the fact bodes at all ill for the private language argument, but my impression is that although it is usually acknowledged that Mises's argument points to a real difficulty for centrally planned economies, it is now almost universally rejected as a theoretical proposition.

Postscript

Wittgenstein and
Other Minds

In his well-known review of *Philosophical Investigations*,[1]
Norman Malcolm remarks that in addition to his 'internal'
attack on private language, Wittgenstein also makes an
'external' attack. "What is attacked is the assumption that once
I know from my *own* case what pain, tickling, or consciousness is, then I can transfer the idea of these things to objects
outside myself (§283)." Traditional philosophy of mind had
argued, in its 'problem of other minds', that given that I know
what it means for *me* to feel a tickle, I can raise the sceptical
question whether others ever feel the same as I do, or even
whether there are conscious minds behind their bodies at all.
The problem is one of the epistemic *justification* of our 'belief'
that other minds exist 'behind the bodies' and that their
sensations are similar to our own. For that matter, we might
equally well ask whether stones, chairs, tables, and the like
think and feel; it is assumed that the hypothesis that they do

[1] Norman Malcolm, "Wittgenstein's *Philosophical Investigations*," *The
Philosophical Review*, vol. 63 (1954), reprinted, with some additions and
revisions, in *Knowledge and Certainty* (Prentice-Hall, Englewood Cliffs,
New Jersey, 1963), pp. 96–129. The paper is also reprinted in Pitcher
(ed.), *Wittgenstein: The Philosophical Investigations*. Page references below
are to the version in *Knowledge and Certainty*.

think and feel makes perfect sense. A few philosophers – solipsists – doubt or positively deny that any body other than one ('my body') has a mind 'back of' it. Some others – panpsychists – ascribe minds to all material objects. Yet others – Cartesians – believe that there are minds behind human bodies, but not those of animals, let alone inanimate bodies. Perhaps the most common position ascribes minds to both human and animal bodies, but not to inanimate bodies. All presuppose without argument that we begin with an antecedently understood general concept of a given material object's 'having', or not having, a mind; there is a problem as to which objects in fact have minds and why they should be thought to have (or lack) them. In contrast, Wittgenstein seems to believe that the very *meaningfulness* of the ascription of sensations to others is questionable if, following the traditional model, we attempt to extrapolate it from our own case. On the traditional model in question, Wittgenstein seems to be saying, it is doubtful that we could *have* any 'belief' in other minds, and their sensations, that ought to be justified.

Malcolm quotes §302: "If one has to imagine someone else's pain on the model of one's own, this is none too easy a thing to do: for I have to imagine pain which I *do not feel* on the model of the pain which I *do feel*. That is, what I have to do is not simply to make a transition in imagination from one place of pain to another. As, from pain in the hand to pain in the arm. For I am not to imagine that I feel pain in some region of his body. (Which would also be possible.)" What is the argument here? Malcolm's first attempt at exegesis is: "If I were to learn what pain is from perceiving my own pains then I should, necessarily, have learned that pain is something that exists only when *I* feel it. This property is essential, not accidental; it is nonsense to suppose that the pain I feel could exist when I did not feel it. So if I obtain my *conception* of pain from pain that I experience, then it will be part of my conception of pain that *I* am the only being that can experience it. For me it will be a *contradiction* to speak of *another's* pain."[2] Subsequently

[2] Malcolm, "Wittgenstein's *Philosophical Investigations*," pp. 105–6.

Malcolm abandoned this argument, denying, under the influence of Wittgenstein's §253, that there is any significant sense according to which only I can feel my own pains.[3] Be this as it may, it is more important – here I speak for myself! – to realize that the principle implied here does not seem to be correct. If I see some ducks for the first time in Central Park, and learn my 'concept' of ducks from these 'paradigms', it may be plausible to suppose that it is impossible ('nonsense', if you will) to suppose that these very ducks could have been born in the fifteenth century. It also may be plausible to suppose that these very ducks could not possibly have come from different biological origins from those from which they in fact sprang. Again, it may be plausible to suppose that if these particular ducks are mallards, *they* could not have failed to be mallards. It by no means follows, whether these essentialist claims are correct or not, that I cannot form the concept of ducks living at a different time, having different genetic origins, or of a different species, from the paradigms I used to learn the 'concept of duck'. That time, origin, and species may have been essential to the original sample is irrelevant. Again, I could learn the word 'blue' if someone points to a particular band of the rainbow. Surely it is essential to *this* particular color patch that it should have been a phenomenon of the atmosphere, not a color patch on the surface of a particular book! There is no reason to conclude that I must, therefore, be unable to apply color terminology to books. The passage quoted from Wittgenstein makes no special mention of 'essential' or 'accidental' properties; it simply seems to imagine a difficulty in imagining 'pain which I *do not feel* on the model of the pain which I *do feel*'. What is the special difficulty in this? Why is it more difficult than imagining ducks which are not in Central Park on the model of ducks which are in Central Park, or ducks that live in the fifteenth century on the model of ducks that live in the twentieth?

Similarly Wittgenstein's famous remarks in §350 seem to

[3] See p. 105, n. 2, of the same paper.

give limited help: ' "But if I suppose that someone has a pain, then I am simply supposing that he has just the same as I have so often had." – That gets us no further. It is as if I were to say: "You surely know what 'It is 5 o'clock here' means; so you also know what 'It's 5 o'clock on the sun' means. It means simply that it is the same time there as it is here when it is 5 o'clock." ' Indeed, if '5 o'clock here' is defined with reference to the position of the sun in the sky, or something related, it will be inapplicable to a place on the sun. If the presuppositions of applicability of 'It's five o'clock here' are violated on the sun, we cannot immediately extend the concept to locations on this heavenly body, in the way we can extend it to distant portions of the earth where these presuppositions are fulfilled. What grounds, however, do we have to suppose that any special presuppositions of the concept 'pain' prevent its extension from me to others? After all, we constantly do apply concepts to new cases to which they have not previously been applied.

Is the sentence I just wrote correct, from Wittgenstein's point of view? Doesn't his sceptical paradox call into question whether we can simply 'extend' such a concept as 'duck' to new cases? For Wittgenstein's sceptic argues, contrary to the naive vein in which I have just been writing, that there is indeed a problem in 'extending' such a term as 'duck' from ducks seen in Central Park to ducks not found there. No set of directions I give myself, the sceptic argues, can mandate what I do in new cases. Perhaps 'duck', as I learned it, meant *duckog*, where something is a duckog if it is a duck and has been in Central Park or is a dog and has never been there . . . In §350, Wittgenstein is concerned to undermine the natural response that to attribute pain to another is simply to suppose "that he has just the same as I have so often had". The final moral of §350 is: "The explanation by means of *identity* does not work here. For I know well enough that one can call 5 o'clock here and 5 o'clock there 'the same time', but what I do not know is in what cases one is to speak of its being the same time here and there. In exactly the same way it is no explanation to say: the supposition that he has a pain is simply the supposition that he has the same as I. For that part of the grammar is quite clear to me: that is, that one will say that the stove has the same experience as I, *if* one says: it is in pain and I am in pain." Now the response attacked in this passage parallels, in an obvious way, one favorite response to Wittgenstein's sceptical doubts of the 'plus'–'quus' type – the response that I simply should go on the 'same way' as before (see §§214–17; and see note 13 above). And the answer that, whether I regard myself as having meant plus or quus, I can say that I 'go on in the same way', is strikingly parallel to §350. So perhaps that section is just one more instance of Wittgenstein's sceptical problem. That imagining the pain of others on the model of my own is 'none too easy a thing to do' would simply be a special case of the more general point that applying *any* concept to a new case is 'none too easy a thing to do'. Or, perhaps, that it is all too easy a thing to do – that I can apply an old term to new cases as I please, unconstrained by any previous intentions or determinations.

Since the attack on sameness, or identity, as a genuine explanation is such a constant theme of Wittgenstein's sceptical argument, I myself would suspect that there is a relationship between §350 and other passages attacking the use of 'sameness'. But it is unlikely that this is the whole of the story. For one thing, the '5 o'clock on the sun' example seems obviously intended as a case where, without the intervention of any arcane philosophical scepticism about rule-following, there really is a difficulty about extending the old concept – certain presuppositions of our application of this concept are lacking. The same is supposed to be true of the example of 'the earth is beneath us' in §351. No doubt an unreflective person may unthinkingly suppose that '5 o'clock' would make sense on the sun, but – so §350 seems to say – reflection on the presuppositions that must be satisfied for our clock system to apply will soon convince him that any extension to the sun is dubious. Wittgenstein's sceptical argument is more radical, claiming that in no case do I give directions to determine future uses, even where there is no ordinary problem as to whether the presuppositions of the application of an old concept are satisfied in new cases. In §302 and §350, Wittgenstein seems to mean that, *waiving* his basic and general sceptical problem, there is a *special* intuitive problem, of the ordinary type illustrated by the '5 o'clock on the sun' example, involved in extending the concept of mental states from oneself to others. In fact, as I will explain shortly, I believe that Wittgenstein's concern with this special problem antedated the last period of his philosophy, when his sceptical problem became prominent.

What can the problem be? What is wrong with the traditional assumption that, given that I have sensations and a mind (or: that my body has a mind 'behind it') I can meaningfully ask whether other material objects have minds 'behind' them? Malcolm, reconsidering his exegesis of Wittgenstein on other minds, concluded that the traditional picture assumed that we had no 'criterion' for attributing minds or sensations to others; but without such a criterion the attribution of minds or sensations would be meaningless.[4] Malcolm seemed to suppose that a 'criterion' for attributing sensations to others was a way of establishing with certainty that they have such sensations. Critics wondered whether the argument rested on dubious verificationist suppositions, and much subsequent discussion has continued within this framework – a framework continuous with much discussion of the private language argument itself. Given the importance of the notion of a criterion to Wittgenstein's later philosophy, this strand of exegesis may have considerable merit.[5] However, I myself

---

[4] See Malcolm, "Knowledge of Other Minds," *The Journal of Philosophy*, vol. 45, (1958), reprinted in *Knowledge and Certainty*, pp. 130–40. See especially pp. 130–2 in the reprint. The paper also appears in Pitcher (ed.), *Wittgenstein: The Philosophical Investigations*. Page references below are to the version in *Knowledge and Certainty*.

[5] It will be clear from my exposition below, however, that I find little direct relation to any argument involving a demand for criteria (as an unargued premise) in the key passages that suggest the difficulty of imagining the sensations of others on the model of my own. No such

believe that a central strand in Wittgenstein's argument in §302 and related passages can be explained without special resort to the notion of a criterion. This strand of the argument, as I see it, rests on no special verificationist premise that to understand the concept of another person's having a sensation we must possess a means of verifying whether he has one. In fact, the main aspects of Wittgenstein's views on the question are already present in his writings, lectures, and conversations in the transitional period between the *Tractatus* and the *Investigations*; in somewhat less explicit form they are present in the *Tractatus* itself. In fact, I think that not only is Wittgenstein's

---

argument is suggested in these passages. It is also clear from the exposition below that 'outward criteria' – in the sense expounded above, pp. 98–107 – play an important role in the *solution* of the difficulty that I seem to be unable to imagine the sensations of others on the model of my own. I think Malcolm's very strong verification principle would need a great deal of elaboration and defense to convince typical present-day readers. Malcolm's targets – those who argue by analogy for other minds – hold that I infer, generalizing from the observed correlation in my own case, that those who behave as I do very probably have minds, thoughts, and sensations like my own. So they do not regard statements about other minds as 'unverifiable'. The relevant principle Malcolm uses against them seems to be: For a statement of a given type to be meaningful, there must be, *as a matter of definition, not the result of inductive reasoning*, a means of deciding *with certainty* whether statements of the given type are true. (See "Knowledge of Other Minds," p. 131.) Those who argue by analogy fall short on the italicized phrases.

In "Knowledge of Other Minds" Malcolm neither argues for this principle nor elaborates on it. Surely the principle needs careful discussion so as to see why it does not rule out, for example, statements about the distant past. More important, even if the principle can be stated so as to be free of obvious counterexamples, most readers would think that it cannot be assumed, but must be argued.

Above (pp. 98–107) we discussed 'criteria' in Wittgenstein's philosophy, arguing that to the extent that one can look at his philosophy as involving anything like a verification principle, the principle must be *deduced*, not assumed as an unargued premise. Nor need any verification principle as strong as the one Malcolm *seems* to presuppose here be accepted. I am not even sure that such a principle is consistent with everything Malcolm himself says elsewhere.

discussion of other minds in the *Investigations* continuous with his earliest thought, it is continuous with one important strand in the traditional treatment of the problem. The basic reasons why Wittgenstein worries that imagining the sensations of others on the model of my own is 'none too easy a thing to do' are both more intuitive and more traditional than are any considerations that might arise from verificationist premises. This much is suggested by the '5 o'clock on the sun' and 'the earth is beneath us' examples – neither makes any special reference to verification or criteria, but only to a conceptual difficulty in applying a concept to certain cases. §302 seems to suggest that there is a comparable intuitive difficulty if I wish to extend the concept of sensation to others on the basis of my own case.

Let me attempt to give the reader a feeling for the difficulty, and for its historical roots. According to Descartes, the one entity of whose existence I may be certain, even in the midst of doubts of the existence of the external world, is myself. I may doubt the existence of bodies (including my own), or, even assuming that there are bodies, that there ever are minds 'behind' them; but I cannot doubt the existence of my own mind. Hume's reaction to this is notorious: "There are some philosophers, who imagine we are intimately conscious of what we call our SELF; that we feel its existence and its continuance in existence; and are certain, beyond the evidence of a demonstration, both of its perfect identity and simplicity. The strongest sensation, the most violent passion, say they, instead of distracting us from this view, only fix it the more intensely, and make us consider their influence on *self* either by their pain or pleasure. To attempt a farther proof of this were to weaken its evidence; since no proof can be derived from any fact of which we are so intimately conscious; nor is there any thing, of which we can be certain, if we doubt of this. Unluckily all these positive assertions are contrary to that very experience, which is pleaded for them, nor have we any idea of *self*, after the manner it is here explain'd . . . For my part, when I enter most intimately into what I call *myself*, I always stumble on some

Hume

particular impression or other, of heat or cold, light or shade, love or hatred, pain or pleasure. I never can catch *myself* at any time without a perception, and never can observe any thing but the perception . . . If any one, upon serious and unprejudic'd reflection, thinks he has a different notion of *himself*, I must confess I can reason no longer with him. All I can allow him is, that he may be in the right as well as I, and that we are essentially different in this particular. He may, perhaps, perceive something simple and continu'd, which he calls *himself*; tho' I am certain there is no such principle in me."[6]

So: where Descartes would have said that I am certain that "I have a tickle", the only thing Hume is aware of is the tickle itself. The self – the Cartesian ego – is an entity which is wholly mysterious. We are aware of no such entity that 'has' the tickle, 'has' the headache, the visual perception, and the rest; we are aware only of the tickle, the headache, the visual perception, itself. Any direct influences from Hume to Wittgenstein are difficult to substantiate; but the Humean thoughts here sketched continued through much of the philosophical tradition, and it is very easy to find the idea in the *Tractatus*. In 5.631 of that work, Wittgenstein says, "There is no such thing as the subject that thinks or entertains ideas. If I wrote a book called *The World as I found it* . . . it alone could *not* be mentioned in that book." Continuing in 5.632–5.633, he explains: "The subject does not belong to the world: rather, it is a limit of the world. Where *in* the world is a metaphysical subject to be found? You will say that this is exactly like the case of the eye and the visual field. But really you do *not* see the eye. And nothing *in the visual field* allows you to infer that it is seen by an eye."

Whether the influence is direct or indirect, here Wittgenstein is under the influence of characteristically Humean ideas on the self, just as in 5.135, 5.136, 5.1361, 5.1362 (and in the paragraphs from 6.362 through 6.372), he writes under the

---

[6] Hume, *A Treatise of Human Nature*, Book I, Part IV, Section VI ("Of Personal Identity"). The quotation is from pp. 251–2 in the Selby-Bigge edition.

influence of Hume's scepticism about causation and induction. Indeed, the denial that I ever find a subject in the world, and the conclusion (5.631) that no such subject exists, is in complete agreement with Hume. The only sign in these passages of deviation from Hume's view comes in the suggestion in 5.632 that in some sense it may be legitimate to speak of a subject after all, as a mysterious 'limit' of the world, though not as an entity in it.[7]

Wittgenstein returned to this theme in several of his writings, lectures, and discussions of the late 1920s and early 1930s, during the period usually regarded as transitional between the 'early' philosophy of the *Tractatus* and the 'late' philosophy of the *Investigations*. In his account of Wittgenstein's Cambridge lectures in 1930–3,[8] Moore reports that Wittgenstein "said that 'just as no (physical) eye is involved in seeing, so no Ego is involved in thinking or in having toothache'; and he quotes, with apparent approval, Lichtenberg's saying 'Instead of "I think" we ought to say "It thinks"' ('it' being used, as he said, as 'Es' is used in 'Es blitzet'); and by saying this he meant, I think, something similar to what he said of the 'eye of the visual field' when he said that it is not anything which is *in* the visual field." In *Philosophical Remarks*, §58, Wittgenstein imagines a language in which "I have a toothache" is replaced by "There is toothache", and, following Lichtenberg, "I am thinking" becomes "It is thinking".[9]

[7] We shall see below that Lichtenberg, who wrote independently of Hume, is a direct influence on Wittgenstein here. No doubt Pitcher (*The Philosophy of Wittgenstein*, p. 147), and Anscombe (*An Introduction to Wittgenstein's Tractatus*, Hutchinson, London, 1959, chapter 13) are right to see a direct influence from Schopenhauer here as well (so Hume's influence comes to Wittgenstein mediated by the links of Kant and Schopenhauer). I should have studied Schopenhauer and Lichtenberg on these questions, and originally intended to, but I haven't done so (more than cursorily). It might have helped exegetically.

[8] G. E. Moore, "Wittgenstein's Lectures in 1930–33," *Mind*, vol. 63 (1954), and vol. 64 (1955), reprinted in G. E. Moore, *Philosophical Papers*, pp. 252–324. The quotation is on p. 309 in the reprint.

[9] See also F. Waismann, *Wittgenstein and the Vienna Circle* (Basil Blackwell, Oxford, 1979), pp. 49–50 (another work, like *Philosophical Remarks*,

Now the basic problem in extending talk of sensations from 'myself' to 'others' ought to be manifest. Supposedly, if I concentrate on a particular toothache or tickle, note its qualitative character, and abstract from particular features of time and place, I can form a concept that will determine when a toothache or tickle comes again. (The private language argument questions whether this supposition really makes sense, but we are supposed to ignore this argument here.) How am I supposed to extend this notion to the sensations of 'others'? What is this supposed to mean? If I see ducks in Central Park, I can imagine things which are 'like these' – here, still *ducks* – except that they are *not* in Central Park. I can similarly 'abstract' even from *essential* properties of these particular ducks to entities like these but lacking the properties in question – ducks of different parentage and biological origin, ducks born in a different century, and so on. (Remember that we are to ignore Wittgenstein's sceptical argument here, and can adopt the 'naive' terminology of 'abstraction' from the paradigm case.) But what can be meant by something 'just like this toothache, only it is not I, but someone else, who has it'? In what ways is this supposed to be similar to the paradigmatic toothache on which I concentrate my attention, and in what ways dissimilar? We are supposed to imagine another entity, similar to 'me' – another 'soul,' 'mind' or 'self' – that 'has' a toothache *just like* this toothache, except that it (he? she?) 'has' it, just as 'I have' this one. All this makes little sense, given the Humean critique of the notion of the self that Wittgenstein accepts. I have no idea of a 'self' in my own case, let alone a generic concept of a 'self' that in addition to 'me' includes 'others'. Nor do I have any idea of 'having' as a relation between such a 'self' and the toothache. Supposedly,

stemming from Wittgenstein's 'transitional' period). The whole of part VI (§§57–66) of *Philosophical Remarks* is also relevant (and see also, e.g., §§71 there).

Compare also Moritz Schlick, "Meaning and Verification," in H. Feigl and W. Sellars (eds.), *Readings in Philosophical Analysis* (Appleton-Century-Crofts, New York, 1949, pp. 146–70), especially pp. 161–8.

by concentrating my attention on one or more particular toothaches, I can form the concept of toothache, enabling me thereby to recognize at later times when "there is a toothache" or "it toothaches" (as in, "it is raining") on the basis of the "phenomenological quality" of toothaches. Although we have expressed this in the Lichtenbergian terminology Wittgenstein commends, "it toothaches" means what we naively would have expressed by "I have a toothache". The concept is supposed to be formed by concentrating on a particular toothache: when something just like this recurs, then "it toothaches" again. What are we supposed to abstract from this situation to form the concept of an event which is like the given paradigm case of "it toothaches", except that the toothache is not "mine", but "someone else's"? I have no concept of a 'self' nor of 'having' to enable me to make the appropriate abstraction from the original paradigm. The formulation "it toothaches" makes this quite clear: consider the total situation, and ask what I am to abstract if I wish to remove 'myself'.

I think that it is at least in part because of this kind of consideration that Wittgenstein was so much concerned with the appeal of solipsism, and of the behavioristic idea that to say of someone else that he has a toothache is simply to make a statement about his behavior. When he considers the adoption of Lichtenberg's subjectless sensation language, attributions of sensations to others give way to expressions like "The body A is behaving similarly to the way X behaves when it pains," where 'X' is a name for what I would ordinarily call 'my body'. This is a crude behaviorist ersatz for imagining the sensations of others on the model of my own: attributing a sensation to A in no way says that something is happening that resembles what happens when I am in pain (or, rather, when it pains). The attraction, for Wittgenstein, of this combination of solipsism and behaviorism, was never free of a certain discontent with it. Nevertheless, during the most verification-ist phase of his transitional period, Wittgenstein felt that it is hard to avoid the conclusion that since behavior is our sole

method of verifying attributions of sensations to others, the
behaviorist formulation is all that I can mean when I make
such an attribution (see *Philosophical Remarks*, §§64–5).

The point comes into sharp relief when we consider many
customary formulations of the problem of other minds. How
do I know, it is said, that other bodies 'have' 'minds' like my
own? It is assumed that I know from my own case *what* a
'mind' is, and what it is for a 'body' to 'have' it. But the
immediate point of the Hume–Lichtenberg criticism of the
notion of the self is that I have no such idea in my own case that
can be generalized to other bodies. I *do* have an idea, from my
own case, of what it is like for there 'to be pain', but I have no
idea what it would be like for there to be a pain 'just like this,
except that it belongs to a mind other than my own'.

Let us return to §350. That passage questions whether we
know what it means to say that 'someone else has pain' on the
basis of my own case. At the end, the example given is that of a
stove: do we know what it means to say of a stove that it is in
pain? As we said above, the traditional view assumes, without
supposing the need of any further justification, that we have a
general concept of an arbitrary material object 'having'
sensations, or, rather, 'having' a 'mind' that in turn is the
'bearer' of the sensations. (The physical object 'has' sensations
in a derivative sense, if it 'has' a 'mind' that 'has' the
sensations.) Now: are we so sure that we understand all this?
As we have emphasized, we have no idea what a 'mind' is.
And do we know what relation is to hold between a 'mind' and
a physical object that constitutes 'having'? Suppose a given
chair 'has' a 'mind'. Then there are many 'minds' in the
universe, only one of which a given chair 'has'. What
relationship is that 'mind' supposed to have to the chair, that
another 'mind' does not? Why is this 'mind', rather than that
one, the one the chair 'has'? (Of course I don't mean: what is
the (causal) *explanation* why in fact the chair 'has' this 'mind'
rather than that? I mean: what relation is supposed to hold
between the chair and one mind, rather than another, that
constitutes its having this mind, rather than that?) For that
matter, why is it the chair as a whole, rather than just its back,

or its legs, that is related to the given mind? (Why not another physical object altogether?) Under what circumstances would it be the back of the chair, rather than the whole chair, that 'has' a given 'mind' and hence thinks and feels? (This is not the question: how would we *verify* that the relation holds, but rather, under what circumstances would it hold?) Often discussions of the problem of other minds, of panpsychism, and so on, simply ignore these questions, supposing, without further ado, that the notion of a given body 'having' a given 'mind' is self-evident.[10] Wittgenstein simply wishes to question whether we really have such a clear idea what this means: he is raising intuitive questions. See, e.g., §361 ("The chair is thinking to itself: . . . WHERE? In one of its parts? Or outside its body; in the air around it? Or not *anywhere* at all? But then what is the difference between the chair's saying anything to itself and another one's doing so, next to it?". . .) or §283 ("Can we say of the stone that it has a soul [or: a mind] and *that* is what has the pain? What has a soul [or: mind], or pain, to do with a stone?").[11]

It is possible to make various attempts to understand the idea of an object – even an inanimate one – 'having' a 'mind' or a sensation without invoking the notions of 'minds' and 'having' themselves. I might, for example, imagine that the physical object I call 'my body' turns to stone while my thoughts, or my pains, go on (see §283). This could be expressed in Lichten-

---

[10] In *Some Main Problems of Philosophy* (Macmillan, New York, 1953), p. 6, Moore says that one of our common sense beliefs is that "acts of consciousness are quite definitely *attached*, in a particular way, to some material objects." *How* 'attached'? In what way to this object, rather than to that? (In fairness to Moore, he says more to answer these questions than many others do. But it is clear from the present discussion that Wittgenstein would not think his answers were satisfactory.)

[11] See above, note 31 in the main text, for the translation of '*Seele*' as 'soul' or 'mind'. In principle this word may be translated either way, but however it is translated, it is important to realize that Wittgenstein is writing about the problem contemporary English speaking philosophers call 'the problem of other minds', and is asking what the question whether the bodies of others 'have' 'minds' *means*. Any other connotation the use of '*Seele*' may have is probably at best secondary.

berg's jargon: There is thinking, or pain, even while such-and-such an object turns to stone. But: "if that has happened, in what sense will the *stone* have the thoughts or the pains? In what sense will they be ascribable to the stone?" Suppose I were thinking, for example, of the proof that π is irrational, and my body turned to stone while I was still thinking of this proof. Well: what relation would my thoughts of this proof have to the stone? In what sense is the stone still 'my body', not just 'formerly my body'? What difference is there between this case and the case where after 'my body' turned to stone, 'my mind switched bodies' – perhaps to *another* stone? Suppose for the moment that after I turn to stone I think only about mathematics. In general, what could connect a thought about mathematics with one physical object rather than another? In the case where my body turns to stone, the only connection is that the stone *is* what my body *has become*. In abstraction from such a prior history, the connection between the thought and the physical object is even harder to spell out: yet if there is a connection, it must be a connection that exists *now*, independently of an imagined prior history.

Actually, in §283 Wittgenstein is concerned with the connection of a pain, a sensation, with the stone. Now if we forget for a moment that sensations are ascribed to a 'mind' that a physical object 'has', and if we think simply of the connection between the sensation and the physical object without worrying about the intermediate links, then in some cases we may still be able to make sense of the connection between a given sensation and a given physical object, even an inert one such as a stone. Pains, for example, are *located*. They are located in the causal sense that damage or injury to a certain area produces the pain. In another causal sense, relief applied to a certain area may alleviate or eliminate the pain. They are also located in the more primitive, non-causal sense in which I *feel* a pain as 'in my foot', 'in my arm', and the like. Very often these senses coincide, but not always – certainly there is no conceptual reason why they must coincide. But: what if they all coincide, and, by all three tests, a certain pain is 'located' in a certain position in a stone? As I understand Wittgenstein, he deals with this particular question in §302, quoted above, where someone else's body, not a stone, is in question. Assuming that I can imagine that a pain is 'located' in another body, does that give a sense to the idea that 'someone else' might be in pain? Recall the Lichtenbergian terminology: if 'there is pain', perhaps 'there is pain in the stone', or 'there is pain in that arm', where the arm in question is not my arm. Why isn't this just to imagine that *I* feel pain, only 'in' the arm of another body, or even in a stone? Remember that 'there is pain' means 'I have pain', with the mysterious subject suppressed: so it would seem that to imagine 'pain in that arm' is to imagine that *I* have pain in the arm of another body (in the way a person who has lost his arm can feel a pain in the area where his arm once was). There is no concept here of *another* 'self' who feels the pain in the stone, or in the other body. It is for this reason that the experiment of ignoring the other 'mind', and trying to imagine a direct connection between the sensation and the body, fails. To repeat some of what was quoted in §302: "If one has to imagine someone else's pain on the model of one's own, this is none too easy a thing to do . . . what I have to do is not simply to make a transition in imagination from one place of pain to another. As from . . . the hand to . . . the arm. For I am not to imagine that I feel pain in some region of his body. (Which would also be possible.)" In the Lichtenbergian jargon, 'there is pain' *always* means that *I* feel pain.

Even if we ignore the Lichtenbergian terminology, the problem can be restated: What is the difference between the case where *I* have a pain in another body, and where that pain in the other body is 'someone else's' pain and not mine? It would seem that this difference can be expressed only by a direct attack on the problems we have just now been trying to evade: what is a mind, what is it for it to 'have' a sensation, what is it for a body to 'have' a mind? The attempt to bypass these intermediaries and deal directly with the connection of the sensation and the physical object fails, precisely because I cannot then define what it means for 'another mind' to have the sensation in a given physical object, as opposed to 'my' having it there. Wittgenstein insists that the possibility that one person might have a sensation in the body of another is perfectly intelligible, even if it never occurs: "Pain behavior can point to a painful place – but the subject of pain is the person who gives it expression" (§302).

Analogous difficulties beset other similar attempts to establish direct links between a stone and a sensation or thought without passing through the intermediate link of a 'mind'. In each case the Lichtenbergian terminology mentioned above dictates that it is I who has the sensation or thought, only 'in the stone'. So far we have concentrated on the case of sensations and 'inanimate' objects (really: physical objects considered simply as such, ignoring whether they are 'animate' or not). Of course a special connection obtains between mind and body in the case of an 'animate' body. Pain leads to 'pain behavior', and in general I 'will' my own actions. So if there is (pain and) pain behavior in another body, or if the actions of another body are 'willed', does this give a meaning – without the need of any notion of another 'self' and its relation to the body – to the idea that someone else (in the other body) might have pains or thoughts, or give rise to actions? Of course ultimately the idea of pain behavior and other bodily actions will be crucial to Wittgenstein's account of the attribution of mental concepts to others. But at the present stage these ideas appear to be of little assistance to us. The case of pain behavior in another body is simply another wrinkle on what has already been said above: granted the Lichtenbergian terminology, to say that there is pain – perhaps in another body – and that it produces pain behavior – perhaps in that same body – is still to say that *I* feel pain, in another body and producing pain behavior in that body. Only the elusive conception of another 'self' and its relation to material object and sensation could give any sense to the idea that it is someone else, 'in' the other body, who has pain.[12,13]

---

[12] In one respect, Wittgenstein seems, as far as I have found, to be devoid of Humean influence. He never considers the Humean idea that two

impressions belong to the same subject when they are united by appropriate (Lockean) relations of memory, causation, temporal contiguity, and so on. There could be various bundles of perceptions connected in this way and, in this sense, various 'selves'.

With the possible exception of the obscure passage *Tractatus*, 5.5421 (see below), which in any case does not appear to be directed primarily at Hume's theory, I know of no discussion of this idea in Wittgenstein, though I easily could have missed one. For Wittgenstein, there is no distinction between imagining a pain and imagining my having a pain. To imagine that I am in pain, I do *not* have to imagine that my pain is connected to anything else by memory, temporal contiguity, or any other relation.

An intuitively strange feature of the Humean view is that it appears to be an accident that 'impressions' are the impression *of* any subject at all. On the proffered analysis, for an impression to be the impression of a 'self' is for it to be connected appropriately to *other* impressions. Since there can be no necessary connections between distinct things, there can be no reason why a given impression should not stand alone. This consequence of the Humean view seems intuitively bizarre: what would a 'floating', 'unowned' impression be? Is it possible to imagine one? Wittgenstein's own early attitude toward these questions seems ambiguous and somewhat obscure. The repudiation of the subject is Humean, and the subject does not survive even as a 'bundle' of perceptions. (*Tractatus* 5.5421 says, "A composite soul [mind] would no longer be a soul [mind]" – which obviously implies that a Humean soul is not really a soul [but wouldn't Hume agree?].) Also, the *Tractatus* accepts Hume's denial of necessary connections between distinct events (6.37, 5.135, 5.136, 5.1361, etc.). On the other hand, as was mentioned above, the subject seems after all to survive in the *Tractatus*, as a 'limit' of the world, which seems to mean that in some sense, experiences are the experiences of this 'limit', even if the limit is neither in the world nor experienced. In *Philosophical Remarks*, §65, Wittgenstein says, "The experience of feeling pain is not that a person 'I' has something. I distinguish an intensity, a location, etc., in the pain, but not an owner." This sounds like a repudiation of the possessor of pain altogether. (Schlick's view (see note 9 in this postscript) – has been called the 'no ownership' view.) On the other hand, immediately after this passage, Wittgenstein asks, apparently incredulously, "What sort of thing would a pain be that no one *has*? Pain belonging to no one at all?"

Of course in our 'language game' of first-person and third-person talk of sensations, as described from the *Investigations* below, talk of 'floating', 'unowned' Humean sensations can play no role.

13 Although the point is ancillary to the main theme, for those who are interested in (and have some prior knowledge of) the *Tractatus*, some

The case of actions and the will has special features. If for the moment we can treat the case of the will as if it were like the case of pain, so that following Hume, we imagine that an 'impression' of willing is correlated with a movement in a human body other than my own, then the same conclusion applies: In Wittgenstein's Lichtenbergian terminology, all that we can imagine in this way is that *my* will should control another body. If, however, we bring in other well-known considerations from the *Investigations*, the situation only worsens. These considerations, which are of a piece with

sketchy remarks about solipsism and the 'limit' of the world in the *Tractatus* may be of interest. Wittgenstein's discussion of solipsism in 5.6 and the paragraphs subordinate to it, immediately follows his discussion of the application of logic in 5.55 and the paragraphs subordinate to 5.55. On the *Tractatus* theory, how are we to determine what objects there are, and how they are permitted to combine to form elementary propositions? The answer cannot follow from general logical considerations alone. These are said to have established (see *Tractatus*, 5 and the subordinate material following it and preceding 5.55) that all propositions are truth functions of elementary propositions, but it is clear that abstract logical considerations alone cannot establish how many objects there are, what objects there are, how the objects are permitted to combine, and (hence) what the elementary propositions are. (See 5.55, 5.551, 5.552.) Nor can the matter be an empirical one. What objects there are, and how they can be combined, constitute the 'substance' and 'fixed form' of the world (2.021, 2.023), which is common to all possible (conceivable) worlds, not just a matter of the way the world actually is, and thus cannot be a matter of contingent, empirical fact (2.022). Thus, on the *Tractatus* doctrine, the answers to these questions belong to the realm of what can be 'shown' (or: made manifest) but cannot be said. How is it shown? By the fact that I, the user of language, use just one of the languages that – as far as the general logical considerations are concerned – are compatible with the scheme of the *Tractatus*. This is *the* language, the only language I understand. What the form and substance of the world is, is shown by what primitive signs there are, what they denote, and how they combine into elementary sentences. Thus I, the user of language, determine the 'limits' of the world. In this sense the world is mine: I, by using a language with just these signs and these possibilities of combinations (the only signs and possibilities I can think) determine it. What is this 'I', the user of language? Not anything in the world, certainly not one thing among others like it, but a 'limit' of the world, as we have seen above.

Wittgenstein's sceptical paradox and especially his criticism of the view that meaning is a special qualitative state, have various facets corresponding to his critique of this view (see pp. 41–53 above). Thus Wittgenstein would point out that the Humean notion of a special 'impression' of willing like that of a headache is chimerical. Further, even if there were an impression of 'willing' as described, its connection with the action willed would appear to be a purely accidental one – nothing in the *quale* of the impression itself would make it a willing of this action rather than that. This point could be reinforced in terms of Wittgenstein's sceptical paradox – a given volition to do one action could be interpreted as a volition to do another, related to the original as quus is to plus. All this makes any attempt to get a grip on the notion that another mind might be 'in' a body even more tenuous than it was before.

In sum, any attempt to imagine a direct connection between a sensation and a physical object without mentioning a 'self' or 'mind' leads me simply to imagine that *I* have a sensation located elsewhere. So we are compelled to contemplate the original mystery: What is a 'mind', what is it for a 'mind' to 'have' a sensation, what is it for a body to 'have' a 'mind'? Here the argument of Hume and Lichtenberg, and the other considerations we have mentioned, say that we have no such notions. As Wittgenstein puts the question in §283, speaking of the ascription of sensations to other bodies: "One has to say it of a body, or, if you like, of a soul [mind] which some body *has*. And how can a body *have* a soul [mind]?"

Enough: As in the case of the problems of the main text, Wittgenstein has presented us with a sceptical problem – it seems impossible to imagine the mental life of others on the model of our own. Is it, therefore, meaningless to ascribe sensations to others, at least in the sense in which we ascribe them to ourselves? Must we be content with a behavioristic ersatz? We said before that Wittgenstein himself at one time was attracted to such pessimistic and solipsistic conclusions. His later philosophy, however, suggests that such conclusions need re-evaluation. Let us abandon the attempt to ask what a 'self' is, and the like; and let us *look*, instead, at the actual *role* ascriptions of mental states to others play in our lives. Thus we may obtain a 'sceptical solution' to our new sceptical paradox.

Some of what we need has already been stated above in the main text; see especially the discussion of how 'pain' and other sensation terminology works on pp. 98ff. above. Nevertheless some recapitulation and elaboration is desirable. In §244, Wittgenstein introduces his well-known account of how, in the case of sensations, "the connection between the name and the thing [is] set up" – "Words are connected with the primitive, the natural expressions of the sensation and learned in their place. A child has hurt himself and he cries: and the adults talk to him and teach him exclamations and, later, sentences. They teach the child new pain-behavior . . . the verbal expression of pain replaces crying and does not describe it." Thus Wittgenstein thinks that avowals of pain are new, more sophisticated pain behavior that adults teach the child as a substitute for the primitive, non-verbal expression of pain. It is a new way that the child *evinces* his pain. At the same time, as was emphasized in the main text, adults reckon the teaching of the child to have been successful precisely when his natural behavioral manifestations (and, perhaps, other cues) would lead them to judge of him that he is in pain. This tendency goes along with the idea that his avowal is a substitute for some of these natural manifestations; we saw in the main text that this tendency is, according to Wittgenstein's view, essential to the idea that the concept of pain is to be ascribed to the child at all. Thus we need no longer worry that each of us attributes pain in two unrelated senses, one applying to 'myself', the other a behavioristic ersatz 'I' apply to 'others'. On the contrary, the first-person avowals would not make sense without the third-person use.

Remember that Wittgenstein does not analyze a form of language in terms of its truth conditions, but rather asks under what circumstances the form is introduced into discourse, and what role, what utility, the practice of so introducing it has.

The circumstances of introducing 'I am in pain' and 'he is in pain' have just been described. I say 'I am in pain' when I feel pain – as a substitute for my natural inclination to groan. 'He is in pain' is said when the behavior of another person is appropriate (though the attribution can be defeated or withdrawn if more information from a wider context comes in). Note that since 'I am in pain' replaces crying, its utterance can serve as a criterion for a third-person attribution of pain to the utterer, just as crying does. Note further that the notion of a criterion is relevant only in the third-person case. An avowal of pain is not made on the basis of any special application of criteria any more than a cry is. In the most primitive case, it *escapes* from the speaker.

These observations give a partial account of our practices of speaking of sensations. Nevertheless, questions remain. First, it looks as if when I say that he is in pain, I *ought* to mean that he is in the same state as I am when I am in pain. It also looks as if I am not really saying this – that if this is what I meant, I could not simply follow a rule that licenses me to say that he is in pain when he behaves in certain ways. Must I not believe that the behavior – somehow – is *evidence* that he really feels the same thing that I feel, on the inside? Do not all the problems and tangles so far discussed threaten to arise again? Here Wittgenstein's scepticism about rules is important. It is not for us to say, on the basis of any *a priori* conceptions – let alone the incoherent one about imagining the sensations of others on the basis of my own discussed above – what it is for me to apply the rules 'in the same way' in new cases. If our practice is indeed to say 'he is in pain' of him in certain circumstances, then that is what determines what *counts* as "applying the predicate 'is in pain' to him in the same way as to myself". We have already seen that the two uses are inextricably bound up with each other in our normal practice – the first-person use could *not* stand on its own. There is no legitimate question as to whether we do the 'right' thing when we apply 'in pain' to others as we do, any more than there is such a question as to whether we are right in proceeding as we do with 'plus'.

Neither scepticism about other minds nor even about the 'inverted spectrum' makes any sense here. This is what we do; other creatures might have acted differently. The point that we no longer give a theory of language in terms of truth conditions, and the sceptical arguments about the meaningfulness of ascriptions of sensation to others, are important. We cannot ask whether – in some sense given by 'imagining the sensations of others on the model of my own' – he really 'feels the same' as I. Nor ought we to worry whether our statements about the sensations of others make it obscure what 'facts' we are looking for. But in no way is the lack of such 'corresponding facts' fatal to the conception of an attribution of sensations to others as meaningful. To see it as meaningful, we look, not for 'corresponding facts', but for the conditions under which we introduce this terminology, and what roles it plays.

But this leads to a further question. So far we have given a rough idea of the conditions under which sensation language is introduced, but what use is this form of language? In particular, why attribute sensations to others? We said that I attribute pain to others when they behave in certain ways. Why should I not simply assert that they behave in these ways? Why – superfluously – have another form of language? It is not enough to say that 'he is in pain' is not superfluous because it is not logically equivalent to any particular assertion about his external behavior. Clearly there is no such equivalence, nor even do my criteria for saying 'he is in pain' entail that he is. For example, he might be pretending. Circumstances surrounding his behavior might lead me to doubt or deny that he really is in pain, even though in the ordinary case I do not doubt this. Nevertheless, the question remains: why have such a locution as 'He is in pain'? Why don't we always rest content with specific descriptions of behavior?

Something further can be said before we answer our question. Often where we attribute psychological states to others, we are in a much better position to describe others in terms of these states than to describe the behavior itself in some neutral terminology that mentions no inner states. We can say that someone looked angry, or upset, but how easy would it be to describe an expression of anger or upset in terminology that makes no mention of the inner, psychological states? (Of course these are examples of emotions, not sensations.) It would be difficult for many of us to give a description of the appropriate facial contours without mentioning the psychological state they express. It would be even more difficult to give the description if it were demanded that it be given in purely geometrical or physical terms. A proposal to replace attributions of mental states with descriptions of behavior would be very difficult for us to carry out, even if other creatures might be able to succeed. These facts certainly say something about the way we see the world, and in particular how we see our fellow humans. Simply put, we see them, not as physical systems, but as human beings. But what, in terms of our lives, does it mean to see them this way?

Wittgenstein's answer is encapsulated in his well-known aphorism, "My attitude toward him is an attitude toward a soul. I am not of the *opinion* that he has a soul" (p. 178). What is the attitude in question, the attitude toward a human being who is not an automaton? How is this attitude revealed in our ascription of sensations to others? In the case of pain, the picture Wittgenstein wishes to sketch is very well known. When we see someone writhing in pain, we pity him. We rush to his aid, we attempt to comfort him, and so on. Our attitude is far from what our attitude would be to a mechanism, even a valuable one, that is undergoing some difficulty or malfunction. Indeed, we might attempt to repair such a mechanism also; but our reasons and attitudes would be essentially distinct from those toward a human being. Who ever comes to the aid of a mechanism, who pities it?

Various remarks Wittgenstein makes might seem to mean that the attitude I exhibit toward a sufferer is primitive, an attitude with a genesis wholly independent of my own experience of pain and a concomitant belief that he 'experiences the same thing that I do'. In §310, as against an objector who thinks that someone's behavior toward a sufferer must indicate a belief "in something behind the outward expression of pain", Wittgenstein simply answers, "His attitude is proof of his attitude." As in the case of 'grasping a concept' as an explanation of various aspects of my verbal behavior (see pp. 96–8 above), Wittgenstein would reject any attempt to 'explain' my attitude and behavior toward a sufferer by a 'belief' about his 'inner state'. Rather, once again the order is to be inverted: I can be said to think of him as having a mind, and in particular as suffering from pain, in virtue of my attitude and behavior toward him, not the reverse. On page 179, Wittgenstein describes a doctor and a nurse who rush to the aid of a groaning patient. If they say, "If he groans, we must give him more analgesic", need they be thought of as suppressing a "middle term" concerning the patient's inner state? "Isn't the point the service to which they put the description of behavior?"

I think that in these passages Wittgenstein does reject any attempt to explain or justify our behavior in terms of a belief about the 'inner state' of the other person. Such an 'explanation' would raise all the problems about other minds rehearsed in the present postscript, as well as all the problems about private rules discussed in the main text. We have seen, further, that Wittgenstein would regard such an 'explanation' as an inversion of the correct order of ideas. Nevertheless, I am inclined not to accept the conclusion I have sometimes heard drawn that for Wittgenstein my inner experience of pain, and my ability to imagine the sensation, play no real role in my mastery of the 'language game' of attributing sensations to others, that someone who has never experienced pain and cannot imagine it but who has learned the usual behavioral criteria for its attribution uses this terminology just as well as I. The important passage here is §300: "It is – we should like to say – not merely the picture (*Bild*) of the behavior that plays a part in the language-game with the words "he is in pain", but also the picture of the pain . . . It is a misunderstanding . . . The image (*Vorstellung*) of pain is not a picture and this image is not replaceable in the language-game by anything that we should call a picture. – The image of pain certainly enters into the language game in a sense; only not as a picture."

I do not really understand fully the contrast Wittgenstein intends between a '*Vorstellung*' and a '*Bild*', rendered by the translator as 'image' and 'picture'. Even less do I have a firm sense of what is meant by the aphorism that follows in §301 – "An image is not a picture, but a picture can correspond to it." In the passages quoted, Wittgenstein gives us no help if we wonder how the 'image' of pain "certainly enters into the language game in a sense", nor does he explain what he wishes to exclude when he denies that it enters into that game "as a picture". Nevertheless, I have at least the following partial sense as to what is meant. Wittgenstein's use of the term 'picture' here is related to his use of it in the *Tractatus* – a picture is to be compared with reality, it says that the external world is in a state corresponding to the picture. To use the image of pain as a picture is to attempt to imagine the pain of another on the model of my own, and to assume that my statement that the other person is in pain is true precisely because it 'corresponds' to this picture. Immediately following the passages just quoted comes the remark cited early in this postscript: "If one has to imagine someone else's pain on the model of one's own, this is none too easy a thing to do: for I have to imagine pain which I *do not feel* on the model of the pain which I *do feel*" (§302). We have already said quite enough in exposition of this passage. If the problems Wittgenstein sees in the attempt to imagine the pain of another on the model of my own are real, they exclude the attempt to use the 'image' of pain as a 'picture'. To use the image as a picture is to suppose that by an appropriate use of this image, I can give determinate truth conditions for the other person's being in pain, and that one need only ask whether these truth conditions 'correspond with reality' to determine whether my statement that he is in pain is true or false.

Wittgenstein rejects this paradigm of truth conditions and pictures in the *Investigations*. We are not to ask for truth conditions, but for the circumstances under which we attribute sensations to others and the role such attribution plays in our lives. How, then, does "the image of pain certainly enter into the language game in a sense" if not "as a picture"? My suggestion is that it enters into the formation and quality of my attitude toward the sufferer. I, who have myself experienced pain and can imagine it, can imaginatively put *myself* in place of the sufferer; and my ability to do this gives my attitude a quality that it would lack if I had merely learned a set of rules as to when to attribute pain to others and how to help them. Indeed, my ability to do this enters into my ability to identify some of the expressions of psychological states – it helps me to identify these simply as expressions of suffering, not through an independent physicalistic description of them. What plays the appropriate role in the formation of my attitude is not a 'belief' that he 'feels the same as I', but an imaginative ability to 'put myself in his situation'. If my conjecture regarding Wittgenstein's cryptic words here is correct, in the *Investigations* Wittgenstein is still close to the thought he expresses in *Philosophical Remarks* when he writes, "When I am sorry for someone else because he's in pain, I do of course imagine the pain, but I imagine that *I* have it" (§65). The Lichtenbergian–Humean problems discussed above prevent me from trying to imagine that another 'self' 'has' the pain in place of 'me', but of course I can imagine that 'there is pain', meaning thereby what I would ordinarily express if I say, 'I am in pain'. When I am sorry for him, I 'put myself in his place', I imagine myself as in pain and expressing the pain.

Compare the situation with that of a child who has been told in detail about the sexual behavior, and perhaps even the accompanying physiological reactions, of adults. Freudian theories about infantile sexuality (and a subsequent latency period) aside, let us suppose that the child has no idea of erotic feelings 'from the inside', that the child neither imagines them nor feels them. Such child could in principle learn a number of behavioral criteria by which he attributes erotic feelings to adults, and he could learn a great deal about the attitudes and reactions that adults have when they perceive that others are expressing erotic feelings. Nevertheless his grasp of erotic expressions, and the concomitant behavior and attitudes accompanying them, will tend to have a crude and mechanical quality that will disappear only when the child is able to enter into this world as one who has the erotic feelings himself. It is harder to imagine this situation in the case of pain sensations, since from earliest childhood few (if any) members of the human race are barred from entering into the imaginative life given by these sensations.

What should we say of someone who perfectly well understands under what circumstances pain is to be attributed to others, who reacts to pain in others in the appropriate way, but who nevertheless is incapable of imagining or feeling pain himself? Does he mean the same as we do if he says of someone else that he is in pain? Probably Wittgenstein's view is that this is a case where we can say what we like, providing we know all the facts. He would differ from us precisely in the way that our ability to imagine pain enters into our own attitude towards sufferers. In this connection, we can consult Wittgenstein's cryptic remarks (or rather, queries) on the subject in §315; compare also his remarks on 'aspect blindness' in pages 213–18 of the second part of the *Investigations*.[14]

Wittgenstein's method in his discussion of the problem of other minds parallels his method in the discussion of rules and private language treated in the main text. Once again he poses a sceptical paradox. Here the paradox is solipsism: the very notion that there might be minds other than my own, with their own sensations and thoughts, appears to make no sense. Once again, Wittgenstein does not refute the sceptic, showing that his doubts arose from a subtle fallacy. On the contrary, Wittgenstein agrees with the sceptic that the attempt to imagine the sensations of others on the model of my own is ultimately unintelligible. Rather Wittgenstein gives a sceptical solution, arguing that when people actually use expressions attributing sensations to others they do not really mean to make any assertion whose intelligibility is undermined by the

[14] For 'aspect blindness', see also note 29 in the text above.

sceptic (solipsist). Once again, we are like "primitive people" who put a false interpretation on the expressions of civilized men (§194). Once again, the correct interpretation of our normal discourse involves a certain inversion: we do not pity others because we attribute pain to them, we attribute pain to others because we pity them. (More exactly: our attitude is revealed to be an attitude toward other minds in virtue of our pity and related attitudes.)

Wittgenstein's sceptical orientation may be even clearer in the present case than in the case of 'following a rule'. For his sympathy with the solipsist is never completely lost. In §403, he says, "If I were to reserve the word 'pain' solely for what I had hitherto called "my pain" . . . I should do other people no injustice so long as a situation were provided in which the loss of the word "pain" in other connections were somehow supplied. Other people would still be pitied, treated by doctors, and so on. It would, of course, be *no* objection to this mode of expression to say: "But look here, other people have just the same as you!" But what should I gain from this new kind of account? Nothing. But after all neither does the solipsist *want* any practical advantage when he advances his view!" In one sense, the passage is directed against the solipsist: his form of account (essentially the Lichtenbergian language that had attracted Wittgenstein in earlier stages of his thought) 'gains nothing'. It would make no difference to the conduct of our lives, and in this sense – the primary criterion for meaningful language in the *Investigations* – it has 'no use'. On the other hand, he is at least as hostile to the 'common sense' opponent of solipsism, the 'realist'. In the previous section, he characterizes the dispute: "For *this* is what disputes between Idealists, Solipsists, and Realists look like. The one party attacks the normal form of expression as if they were attacking a statement; the others defend it, as if they were stating facts recognized by every reasonable human being." (Does he have Moore's 'defense of common sense' in mind as the second party?) Wittgenstein denies that there is any fact – 'recognized by every reasonable human being' – that the solipsist wrongly doubts or denies (in this case, the fact that 'other people have just the same as you'). Neither a notation that makes it appear as if others 'have the same as I' nor a notation that makes it appear as if they do not is *forced* on us by an independent set of objective 'facts of the matter'. Moreover, although Wittgenstein thinks we 'gain nothing' from the solipsist's form of expression, and rejects his imputation that the normal form of expression is at all in error, it seems clear that Wittgenstein still thinks that the solipsist's terminology illuminates an important philosophical truth obscured by the normal mode of expression.

Wittgenstein's scepticism – the gulf that separates him from 'common sense philosophy' – is apparent. For the natural response of common sense philosophy is that the solipsist *is* wrong, since others *do* have the same sensations as he. In the parallel discussion of this point in *The Blue Book* (p. 48), Wittgenstein distinguishes the 'common sense philosopher', from the 'common sense man, who is as far from realism as from idealism'. The common sense philosopher supposes that 'surely there is no difficulty in the idea of supposing, thinking, imagining that someone else has what I have'. Here Wittgenstein reminds us of Berkeley once again – is the common sense philosopher really to be distinguished from the common sense man in this way? The solipsist's terminology illuminates the truth that I *cannot* imagine someone else's pain on the model of my own, and that there *is* something special about my use of 'I am in pain' – I do not simply apply a predicate to an object called 'myself' among other objects (not even to a human being among other human beings). 'I am in pain' is supposed to be a sophisticated substitute for groaning; and when I groan, I refer to no entity, and attribute no special state to any. Here it is noteworthy that the problem of 'self-consciousness' – brought to the fore of recent philosophical discussion by Hector-Neri Castañeda[15] – already appears in Wittgenstein.

[15] See H.-N. Castañeda, "'He': A Study in the Logic of Self-Consciousness," *Ratio*, vol. 8 (1966), pp. 130–57; "On the Logic of Attributions of Self-Knowledge to Others," *The Journal of Philosophy*, vol. 54 (1968),

Castañeda emphasizes that 'Jones said that he was hungry' does *not* mean 'Jones said that Jones was hungry', for Jones need not realize that he is Jones. The same holds if 'Jones' is replaced throughout by a definite description, such as 'Smith's secretary': Smith's secretary need not realize that he is Smith's secretary, either. See §404: "Now in saying this [I am in pain] I don't name any person. Just as I don't name anyone when I *groan* with pain. Though someone else sees who is in pain from the groaning . . . What does it mean to know *who* is in pain? It means, for example, to know which man in this room is in pain: for instance, that it is the one who is sitting over there, or the one who is standing in the corner, the tall one over there with the fair hair, and so on . . . Now which of them determines my saying that 'I' am in pain? None." Continuing in §405: " "But at any rate when you say, 'I am in pain', you want to draw the attention of others to a particular person." – The answer might be: "No, I want to draw their attention to *myself*." " At least a partial exegesis of §405 would be: When I say, 'I am in pain', I do not mean to draw the attention of others to a person *identified* in any particular way (e.g. identified as 'the one who is standing in the corner'), but I draw attention to myself in the same way that if I groan I draw attention to myself. Thus others, hearing the groan, will say "Jones is in pain", "the person in the corner is in pain", and the like, if I am Jones, or the person in the corner. But I do not identify myself in this way; I may not even know whether I am Jones or the person in the corner, and, if I do my knowledge is irrelevant to my utterance. Thus the first person pronoun, for Wittgenstein, is to be assimilated neither to a name nor to a definite description referring to any particular person or other entity. In the *Tractatus*, Wittgenstein bases his account of the self on the Hume–Lichtenberg thought experiment, arriving at his conception of the subject as a rather

---

pp. 439–56. Castañeda has written extensively on the problem, and there are many papers by others. Peter Geach and G. E. M. Anscombe are two authors who have written on the problem (presumably) under the specific influence of Wittgenstein.

mysterious 'limit of the world', which 'does not belong to the world' and 'shrinks to an extensionless point' (5.632; 5.64). In the *Investigations*, the special character of the self, as something not to be identified with any entity picked out in any ordinary manner, survives, but it is thought of as deriving from a 'grammatical' peculiarity of the first person pronoun, not from any special metaphysical mystery. Clearly much more needs to be said here: a few sketchy and allusive remarks on the analogy between 'I am in pain' and a groan hardly give a complete theory, or even a satisfying picture of our talk of ourselves. But here I will not attempt to develop the subject further. [16]

[16] For Wittgenstein's views on this subject, in addition to the material quoted above, see *The Blue Book*, pp. 61–5. The surrounding pages have much material relevant to the problems of this postscript.

[87] If Wittgenstein had been attempting to give a necessary and sufficient condition to show that '125', not '5', is the 'right' response to '68+57', he might be charged with circularity. For he might be taken to say that my response is correct if and only if it agrees with that of others. But even if the sceptic and I both accept this criterion in advance, might not the sceptic maintain that just as I was wrong about what '+' meant in the past, so I was wrong about 'agree'? Indeed, to attempt to reduce the rule for addition to another rule – "Respond to an addition problem exactly as others do!" – falls foul of Wittgenstein's strictures on 'a rule for interpreting a rule' just as much as any other such attempted reduction. Such a rule, as Wittgenstein would emphasize, also describes what I do wrongly: I do not consult others when I add. (We wouldn't manage very well, if everyone had to follow a rule of the proposed form – no one would respond without waiting for everyone else.)

What Wittgenstein *is* doing is describing the utility in our lives of a certain practice. Necessarily he must give this description in our own language. As in the case of any such use of our language, a participant in another form of life might apply various terms in the description (such as "agreement") in a non-standard 'quus-like' way. Indeed, we may judge that those in a given community 'agree', while someone in another form of life would judge that they do not. This cannot be an objection to Wittgenstein's solution unless he is to be prohibited from any use of language at all. (A well-known objection to Hume's analysis of causation – that he presupposes necessary connections between *mental* events in his theory – is in some ways analogous.)

Many things that can be said about one individual on the 'private' model of language have analogues regarding the whole community in Wittgenstein's own model. In particular, if the community all agrees on an answer and persists in its view, no one can correct it. There can be no corrector *in* the community, since by hypothesis, all the community agrees. If the corrector were outside the community, on Wittgenstein's view he has no "right" to make any correction. Does it make any sense to *doubt* whether a response we all agree upon is 'correct'? Clearly in some cases an individual may doubt whether the community may correct, later, a response it had agreed upon at a given time. But may the individual doubt whether the community may not in fact *always* be wrong, even though it never corrects its error? It *is* hard to formulate such a doubt within Wittgenstein's framework, since it looks like a question, whether, as a matter of 'fact', we might always be wrong; and there is no such fact. On the other hand, within Wittgenstein's framework it is still true that, for me, no assertions about community responses for all time need establish the result of an arithmetical problem; that *I* can legitimately calculate the result for myself, even given this information, is part of our 'language game'.

I feel some uneasiness may remain regarding these questions. Considerations of time and space, as well as the fact that I might have to abandon the role of advocate and expositor in favor of that of critic, have led me not to carry out a more extensive discussion.

Index